T4-AQK-135

KID-TV

Rock Video
Strikes Again

Barbara Adams

A YEARLING BOOK

Published by
Dell Publishing Co., Inc.
1 Dag Hammarskjold Plaza
New York, New York 10017

Yearling ® TM 913705, Dell Publishing Co., Inc.

ISBN: 0-440-47170-2

Printed in the United States of America

December 1986

10 9 8 7 6 5 4 3 2 1

CW

Rock Video

Strikes Again

Chapter 1

I, MINNIE O'REILLY, was in the middle of a truly terrible day.

It all started going wrong even before I woke up. First I slept through the alarm clock. Then I lost my homework somewhere in my room. I agree that's hard to understand since my room is as neat as a pin in spite of my mother's saying it looks like a trash heap.

Because I was looking for my homework, I missed breakfast, so I looked for something to eat on the bus—and missed the bus.

I had to ask my mother to drive me to school, which made her angry. I was late anyway, because the car wouldn't start. I forgot my lunch money, so I had to borrow some from Ron the Dumb— he's my big brother with the small mind. Finally, to put the icing on the cake, we had a surprise test in math and I hate surprises.

See what I mean? Not a great day.

But I decided things would get better. I even got to the KID-TV studio right after school with no problems! I crossed my fingers and hoped that my luck was on the upswing. That was when Jamie Burns told me I had to handle camera two because Jeannie had impetigo.

Could I get impetigo from a television camera?

I like being camera person. There are lots of great things you can do with a camera—like focus on someone's left eye, or the top of someone's head. Or center it directly on the nose and mouth of someone who is talking. No. Really, I'm pretty good on camera. Jeannie is better, of course, but she's had more practice.

"One minute to air time!" Jamie yelled. I focused in on Lance Larchmont. He was about to do the news.

Jamie Burns is the station manager of KID-TV, and she's the greatest living human in Wellsburg— or maybe even anywhere. KID-TV is the cable station that was given to us kids at Wellsburg Junior-Senior High School. It was partly to keep the station going, and partly to see if we could provide socially redeeming shows for the young. Rufus Z. Wells, who donated the funding, wants to shut us down.

He says we're incompetent nincompoops. He tries every now and then to catch us doing something wrong, but we're too smart for him—most of the time.

The thing I like about ol' R. Z.—who happens to be my friend Billy's uncle—is that he's modest. In an effort to avoid looking too stuck-up, he has named everything he owns—which is practically everything in town—after himself.

But enough about R. Z. Wells.

"A water main break on Bridge Street closed the downtown area to motorists for three hours earlier today," Lance the anchorperson said, rolling his eyes and trying to look grim, "but police and maintenance workers now have the situation under control."

Too bad it didn't happen during the morning rush, I thought. That way I would never have gotten to school at all. Some days it's better to be in a traffic jam. Oh, well.

"And on the brighter side," Lance continued, with an idiotic grin on his face, "Melanie Frobisher of Highland Heights found a lost dog last night. After returning the dog to its owner, she received a one-hundred-dollar reward. Why such gratitude? Fifi, the wandering Lhasa apso in question, is a prize-winning show dog. Her owners were delighted to have her back in time for the dog show in

Madison Square Garden in New York City day after tomorrow.

"So-o-o-o-o-o . . . . . Eat your hearts out, all you other mutts. Second prize is the best you can get this year! Fifi's back for all the blue ribbons!"

I heard a groan behind me and turned around in time to see Mike McGee holding his head. Lance was doing it again. Mike wrote the news, and Lance was always complaining that it was too dry and boring. Lance sometimes added comments to liven the news up. This was one of those times.

Pretty lively stuff, Lance.

After that, things went smoothly. Billy did the weather . . . and we got treated to a rundown of the temperatures in Bangkok, Pago Pago, Inner Mongolia, and Cleveland. Kathy Nelligan did an enthusiastic sports wrap-up, and Sandra Andrews did her Ms. Lonelyhearts Advice to the Lovelorn. She reads letters people have written in, and then gives them advice. This is a very popular part of the show, because everyone who writes the letters uses made-up names, and everyone else tries to guess who wrote the letters. It makes for some exciting gossip.

Then it was time for Muffin Prendergast's aerobics show. Muffin's show offers great possibilities for creative camera work, but we're not allowed to do things like focus in on her rear end or her

4

feet—or her ears. Too bad. Muffin Prendergast think's she's a great gift to mankind. Heavy on the *man*, light on the *kind*.

Muffin used to date my big brother Ron, but not anymore, thank goodness. It was bad enough having to spend every afternoon around her, but most evenings, too? Ron is seventeen and I'm twelve, and we don't have a great relationship.

If Ron and Muffin are examples of what being a teenager is like, I think I'll stay twelve. Being a teenager appears to be roughly like instant brain death.

Muffin was just launching into a hair-raising leg lift when Rock Video came barreling into the studio, waving and flapping his arms. This was odd, because Rock—and I feel I must tell you that this is not his real name—is normally in control of his arms and legs. Something awful must have happened.

Muffin stopped for a second, but then she went right on. An earthquake under City Hall couldn't have been more important than her show. Anyway, I just held the camera on her and tried to hear what Rock was babbling about.

Rock Video is otherwise known as Horace Wigglesworth, and he is rich. He was given his own VCR and video camera for Christmas, which means that he is our latest addition to the KID-TV staff.

You see, Rock makes his own rock videos. He came to Jamie about two months ago and offered to put together a rock video show for us. Jamie thought it was great. So did everyone else, but I have to tell you, the videos are a little weird.

Mostly, they seem to be home movies of Rock's friends who have their own bands. The bands aren't too bad, but the videos are strange. They have stuff like—well, let me give you an example.

There's this group of kids at school who have a band they call The Weirdos. The Weirdos don't write new songs, but they play other, more famous groups' music pretty well. The video that Rock made has the whole band sitting at a big picnic table out by Wells Lake Recreation Plaza. There are mounds of food on the table, and during the video the band members stuff their faces with food, getting it all over the table, all over themselves, all over the grass, and finally all over the lens of the camera. They eat in time to the music.

Now Rock was babbling and gasping for breath, Jamie's eyes were getting really round and big, and I heard the name Simon Gear.

Simon Gear! Simon Gear is the most famous, the most incredible, the most terrific hunk of a rock star anyone ever heard of. Not that I, personally, think he's a hunk, you understand. But every other girl in Wellsburg seems to. I'm merely reporting the facts.

Jamie whispered to Charlie on camera one, and then ran back to Lance. Lance was sitting at the news desk with his feet up, picking his teeth. Jamie shoved a piece of paper under his nose. The monitor switched from a terrific shot of Muffin doing leg lifts to one of Lance staring at the piece of paper. His mouth was open.

Muffin, who always keeps one eye on the monitor, stopped in mid-lift and glowered at Jamie. But only for a minute. Like the rest of us, she stared openmouthed at Lance as he made his announcement.

"Er . . . uh . . . Ladies and gentlemen, I was just handed this news bulletin. . . . Er . . . It appears that information has just been received by KID-TV that . . . I can't believe this"— Lance was beginning to wheeze—"that SIMON GEAR . . . oh, my gosh . . . the great rock star Simon Gear is going to be appearing in Wellsburg next Saturday night for a homecoming concert!"

Homecoming? I thought. Since when is Wellsburg Simon Gear's home?

"That's right, all you rock fans out there in KID-TV land. I guess that can only mean one thing! Simon Gear is from Wellsburg! Our hometown is HIS hometown! And he'll be here next Saturday night!"

Muffin screamed, and there were scattered cheers and clapping from the staff. Jamie signaled to me, and I cut back to Muffin, who was holding her face and crying. Incredible. But anyway, as she howled "I can't believe it, I can't believe it," she finished her leg lifts.

After that it was time to wrap up the KID-TV segment and go into the movie. Lennie Farini—who I'm told is our very own, personal hunk—was ready to go. He put on a terrific film about the Royal Canadian Mounted Police. Then he joined us all in the studio.

If ever it was time for a meeting, this was it! What a break this was going to be!

Chapter 2

"WHADDAYA MEAN, HOMECOMING concert?" Lennie said. "If Simon Gear grew up right here in Wellsburg, then how come nobody knows him?"

We were all sitting around the studio. We always had a meeting after we went off the air. It was part of the way we figured out what we were going to do next, and what we'd already done that needed fixing up. But everyone was so excited about the concert, it was hard to concentrate.

"He's older than we are," Mike answered.

"So what? I know lots of people older than we are," Lennie said. "Not one of them ever mentioned knowing Simon Gear."

"You hang out with a different crowd, Lennie," Dave Madison put in. "Even people like Simon

Gear wouldn't be caught dead knowing those little crooks."

"Stuff it, crumb," Lennie said. Even though his eyebrows were making him look angry, he had a smile on his face.

Dave had just come in from the office, where he had been looking over the ads he'd lined up for tomorrow's show. Dave was trying to get more advertising so we could buy some more new equipment. We finally managed to get a new portable video camera. But both of our studio cameras were held together by paper clips, rubber bands, and orange juice cans.

Fixer—the kid who fixed everything that needed fixing (which was everything we had)—could only do so much. Sooner or later, the cameras were going to crumble to dust. The bets were on for sooner.

"I bet he changed his name," Muffin sniffed in that snooty way she has. She always talked to us the way you'd talk to three-year-olds. Not many people were fond of that habit.

"Changed his name from what?" Billy asked. "Even if he changed his name, he'd still look like himself, wouldn't he?"

"Who knows, these days," Rock Video said. "Maybe he was a little skinny kid who wore glasses and had pimples. Maybe he didn't have any friends."

10

ROCK VIDEO STRIKES AGAIN

Rock was giving a perfect description of himself, which was pretty funny. I guess he figured he'd grow up to look like Simon Gear, and be famous, and have groupies. Good luck, Horace.

"But whether or not any of us knew him when he lived here is beside the point," Rock continued.

"Rock is right," Jamie said. I winced at the sound of that. "The real point is that Simon Gear is coming to Wellsburg—his hometown—next Saturday for a concert. We have a big job ahead of us. We have to get everyone in Wellsburg ready for this concert, and we have to find out as much as we can about Simon Gear."

"How are we going to do that?" Lennie asked, uncurling himself from his chair. "Are we going to ask everyone in the whole city if they know who he *really* is?"

"What a great idea!" Willow said. "That's *exactly* what we'll do. Oh, Lennie, I knew you'd come up with the answer!"

Willow Eichenberry is the second greatest person in Wellsburg. She's our roving reporter, and she's really, really smart. I bet when she grows up she's going to be the anchorwoman of her own news show. And she's pretty too. But does she use her smarts when it comes to boys?

Nope. She's crazy about Lennie Farini.

Lennie wears tight black jeans, a black sweatshirt,

11

black boots. He drives a black motorcycle. He reports to his parole officer every week like a good boy. He's a good kid, but Willow deserves better.

"We only have a week, Willow," Jamie said. "How are we going to ask everyone in Wellsburg . . ."

"Easy!" Willow said. "We'll ask them on the air. It'll be part of the news, it'll be part of every station break. I can ask people on the street their opinions. It'll be a great way to drum up excitement for the concert."

"That's right. We can ask people to call in," said Billy. "It would be like those phone-in radio shows where people ask questions. Kids would really love it. We could have every kid in Wellsburg out searching for Simon Gear's real name and family."

"Maybe we could give a reward for information leading to Simon Gear's real name," Jamie said. "Free tickets to the concert!"

"I have an idea!" Muffin said.

Dave Madison, who was looking more and more annoyed as he watched Jamie and Willow act like nits over Lennie's idea, perked up. "Yeah," he said. "Let some of the rest of us give our ideas too. We can't just spend the entire three hours we're on the air asking folks the same stupid question."

"Thank you, Dave," Muffin said with her nose up in the air. "My idea is simply this. For the next week I'll do all my aerobics shows to Simon Gear music. What a trip!"

"Not bad," Jamie said. "I think that's a very good idea, too, Muffin. Do you have all his records?"

"Of *course* I have all his records," Muffin sniffed.

"I also had a thought," said Sandra Andrews. "On my Ms. Lonelyhearts Show, I could ask viewers to send me their love letters to Simon Gear, and I'll make sure he gets them the night of the concert." Actually, Sandy only reads the letters and stuff on the show. John Miller, the world's shyest human being, writes the answers. He's really funny and smart on paper. But if you turned a camera on him, he'd probably die of stage fright.

"You might get some real winners in there," Lennie said. "Would you let me read them first?"

"No," Sandy snapped. "I will *not* let you read them first. My relationship with my viewers is like that of lawyer and client, priest and penitent. I am sworn to protect their right to privacy."

"Until death?" I asked.

Lennie guffawed. "No, until she gets the best offer."

"Stop picking on each other," Jamie said. "That's a great idea, Sandy. Anyone else?"

"I bet I'll be able to get a lot of ads if I can promise that KID-TV will have an exclusive interview with Simon Gear the day of the concert,"

Dave said. "But you guys will have to deliver the goods."

"I can do better than that," Rock Video said, jumping up and down.

Rock is skinny and paces a lot. It gives his videos a lot of vitality, if you know what I mean.

"I'll make *two* videos of Simon Gear. One will be about his arrival—you know, setting up the concert, settling into his hotel room, talking things over with us, conferring with his manager and promoters, rehearsing his group . . . stuff like that. The second one will be of the concert itself. We'll have an exclusive! KID-TV will be the only TV show with Simon Gear's concert on it!"

"It better be," said Dave, standing up and dusting off his jacket, "because I'm going to sell a lot of advertising, and I'll look pretty dumb if we have the kind of messed-up programming we normally have around here."

"You'll look pretty dumb no matter what you do," said Lennie.

Dave snapped around and stared at Lennie. "Listen, you small-time hood. I'd be insulted by that remark if you had any brains at all. But you don't know the first thing about smart. You think you're so cool with those stupid clothes you wear. Your hair is greasy, and you're just the kind of punk who'll never amount to anything. The reason you hang out with crooks is because they're too stupid to figure out what a loser you really are!"

"Dave!" Jamie gasped.

Lennie stood up slowly. He turned around and started walking out of the studio. Willow was up half a second later, and she caught his arm just as he got to the door.

"Let go of me, Willow," he said softly.

"Lennie, don't let him get to you," Willow pleaded.

"He didn't get to me," Lennie said, shaking off Willow's hand. "But I'll tell you what does get to me. I'm sick of all you stupid little kids. I'm sick of listening to your stupid ideas, and most of all, I'm sick of having to spend every afternoon here with a bunch of babies. I quit. That's right, you heard me. As of right now, I QUIT!"

Lennie stormed out of the studio. The door slammed so hard behind him, it shook a cloud of dust off the backdrops rolled up against the wall. Mike started sneezing. He's allergic to everything.

"He'll be back," Dave said, as the rest of us sat around, stunned. "Don't forget, his parole officer makes him come here."

The door banged open again, and Lennie stuck his head inside. "And don't think I'll be back, either. My parole officer will help me find another after-school job. One that pays! We've been talking about that for a long time, and I guess now is when I make it happen!"

The door slammed shut once more, sending another dust shower over us.

"Now look what you've done, Dave," Willow yelled. "You made Lennie quit, and all because you can't keep your big mouth shut!"

That's when I had a horrible thought.

"That's not all he did," I said. "Lennie we could live without. But a driver for the van we can definitely *not* live without."

Jamie groaned. "That's right, Minnie. The van. No one has a license to drive except Lennie. No Lennie, no van."

"How am I going to do the Roving Reporter spot?" Willow said. Her voice came out a wail.

"That shouldn't be a problem," said Dave. "We have the new portable camera pack. Forget about Lennie. Who needs him?"

"I do," Willow said. "Have you ever tried to ride a bike with a portable camera pack? And that also means I can only do taped stuff. I won't be able to do live on-the-scene reports if I haven't got the equipment in the van. Oh, Dave, how could you!"

"Maybe Lennie will change his mind," Billy said, trying to sound cheerful.

"I hope so," said Jamie.

16

ROCK VIDEO STRIKES AGAIN

I didn't think that would happen. Lennie really was out of place in the studio. Not so much because he was different, but because everyone acted as if he were different.

It was as if once he'd gotten into trouble, he'd been branded. Dave was always picking on him about it. I always thought Lennie didn't care; he was always being so snotty about it. But now I wondered.

Chapter 3

WELL, THERE WAS nothing more anyone could do, and it was getting late. So I decided to go home.

At least I, personally, could be the one to tell Ron the great news. One thing Ron really hates is if I know something before he does. I was feeling really great, just thinking about the look on his face when I told him about Simon Gear.

Willow decided to walk home with me. Usually she waits and walks with Jamie because they're best friends. But Jamie was staying at the station for another half hour.

Willow looked terrible. I couldn't ignore it.

"Willow, is there something wrong?" I asked.

"Lennie." That was all she said. I knew what was going to follow—or at least I was pretty sure.

"He'll be back," I said, trying to sound con-

18

vinced. "He knows we need him to drive the van."

"That's not enough," Willow said. "Just because KID-TV needs Lennie, doesn't mean Lennie needs KID-TV, you know."

She had a point.

"And I need Lennie too," she said. I thought she was about to cry. "But he doesn't even know I exist."

"Don't be silly, Willow. Of course he knows you exist! You go on the van with him every day! Who do you think he thinks is back there? The Incredible Hulk?"

"I might just as well be the Invisible Hulk, for all the difference it makes to Lennie Farini," Willow moaned. "Oh, Minnie! He's so gorgeous! He's so perfect! He's so sensitive!"

Aaargh, I thought. But I kept it to myself.

"None of you guys understand Lennie, but he really needs to have someone love him. That's why he tries so hard to be tough. He's a sensitive, kind-hearted boy who's had a very hard life."

"Well," I said, trying to sound as if I meant it, "*you* love him. That should be enough."

"It would be," Willow said, sniffling a little. "But Lennie doesn't *know* that I love him. I was going to try and figure out a way to let him know, but now it's too late!"

19

Then Willow started wailing, and I felt crumbly inside. Love must be pretty horrible, I thought, if it makes you feel like *that*!

"He'll never come back," Willow sobbed. "Nobody at the station was nice to him . . . ever! Dave picks on him all the time. Even though he's older than we are, everyone treats him like garbage. Everyone thinks they're better than Lennie because . . . because . . ."

"I know why," I said slowly, as it dawned on me what had happened. "We all think we're better than he is because we all come from nice families. The worst trouble we ever get into is not handing our homework in on time. Our parents all help us with everything. I bet no one ever helps Lennie with anything, right?"

"Right," said Willow. "Remember when he got in trouble last time?"

We had all assumed that Lennie was guilty when equipment from the station had been stolen. But it turned out he was innocent.

"When he was in jail, no one came to see him. It took his mother forever to bail him out! I couldn't believe it. It was almost as if he had no family at all!"

"I wonder how that feels?" I asked. "I mean, having no family to help you when you really need it."

20

"I don't know," said Willow. "But it must feel awful."

"Yeah," I said. "*Really* awful."

For a moment there I almost had kindly thoughts about Ron. But when we got in front of my house, I saw his bicycle sticking out of the azalea bushes. That's when I remembered how creepy he is, and got a grip on myself.

"Don't worry, Willow," I said. "I'm positive he'll be back soon."

"Oh, Minnie," Willow said, as she waved good-bye to me. "I hope you're right."

"I know I'm right," I said. But as I watched her walk down the block to her house, I wasn't so sure. Then I stepped over Ron's bike, went up the walk, and opened the porch door.

When I got into the house, I headed straight for the kitchen as usual. My mother was in there looking gloomy. She was holding an armful of calamine lotion and little tubes and bottles of ointment.

"What's up, Mom?" I asked, getting a spoonful of peanut butter out of the jar. "Have you been weeding in the poison ivy again?"

One time, my mother cleared out a whole patch of poison ivy by mistake. She had so much calamine lotion on her for the two weeks after that, she looked like a large, pink lollipop.

"No, Minnie," she said pushing open the swing-

21

ing door with her hip. "Your poor brother has come down with the chicken pox. They sent him home from school this afternoon."

"You mean Ron?" I asked.

"He's the only brother you have, if I'm not mistaken," she said. The swinging door swung shut and I had to follow her out into the dining room to finish asking questions. Ron with the chicken pox? Amazing.

"But I just saw him at lunchtime," I said as I followed her up the stairs. "He didn't look or act like someone with the plague."

"Chicken pox is not the plague," my mother said. She opened the door to Ron's room and went in. I went right behind her. This I had to see.

It was true. The curtains were pulled, and it was dark in there. But not too dark to see that Ron's face looked like a polka-dot plate.

"Hey, Ron," I said, trying to cheer him up. "Are you sure you just don't have a rip-roaring case of pimples? Maybe I'll get Dave Madison to get you a lifetime free supply of Zitzoff's Miracle Pimple Cream."

"Go jump in the lake, Minnie," he replied. "And don't forget you owe me a dollar."

"How sick could he be, Mom?" I asked. "He's still thinking about money."

Mom sat down next to Ron and put her hand on his forehead. She looked worried. "I want to take your temperature again, darling." she said. "I think it's gone even higher than it was when you got home."

She stood up and got the thermometer out of her apron pocket. After shaking it down, she stuck it in Ron's mouth. Then she started smoothing his hair away from his forehead. She was doing a real sickbed routine.

Mom's really good when you're sick. That's the only good thing about being sick—Mom makes you tasty little treats to encourage you to eat and get better. Also, you don't have to go to school.

Then Mom turned toward me. "Poor Ron," she said, shaking her head. "The school nurse called me this afternoon saying he had a temperature of one hundred and one. I only hope it doesn't go any higher tonight. But chicken pox does that, you know."

"Aren't you supposed to get chicken pox in the second grade?" I asked. It was just the kind of innocent question that makes Ron go crazy.

"Most children do," Mom said, still stroking his polka-dot cheek. "But I guess Ron didn't. I could have sworn he had the chicken pox, but who knows. Maybe it was the measles that he had, or the German measles. I'll have to look it up."

"I got them in the second grade, right?" I asked.

"I really don't remember, Minnie," my mom said. "But I suppose I'd better go look on your medical record card too. After all chicken pox is contagious. If you didn't already have it, you will soon."

I had this sudden, strong desire to get out of Ron's room.

Out in the hall, I thought for a moment. What did Mom mean, she can't remember? What are mothers for, anyway? They're supposed to have stuff like that tattooed on the inside of their eyelids so they can look it up every time they blink.

And what did she mean, if I didn't have it already, I'd have it very soon? Chicken pox? I didn't want to get the chicken pox! Not now. Not with Simon Gear coming to town and everything.

Then I remembered I hadn't told Ron about the concert yet. Boy, would that burn him up. A Simon Gear concert right here in Wells Memorial Stadium, and he couldn't go! I opened the door to his room a crack and yelled in, "Guess what, Ron? Simon Gear's having his homecoming concert in town next Saturday night! Guess you'll have to sit this one out since you've got the plague. You poor, poor thing!"

As I slammed the door shut, I heard a howl of rage and pain come from in there.

24

I went back down to the kitchen to see what was on for dinner. But there wasn't anything in the oven, in the microwave or in the crockpot. I decided I'd better have a glass of milk and a banana. Then I called Jamie to tell her about poor, poor Ron.

I thought she'd laugh herself silly. Jamie and Ron were going steady for a while there. That was back before he started dating Muffin. But Ron gave Jamie a hard time about being station manager of KID-TV, so she told him to go fly a kite. Wise move, I thought. After all, Jamie was a smart girl.

She didn't know all the disgusting things about Ron that I knew, so it was possible for her to make a mistake about him. But not for long. I'd been about to tell her how he wears his socks to bed and never cleans his ears, but she broke up with him, so I didn't have to. Anyway, I called her up to give her the good news.

But was I ever in for a surprise.

"Oh, no," Jamie said. "Poor Ron. Does he feel awful? Is there anything I can do? Maybe I'd better come right over."

"No, no," I said quickly—as soon as I'd gotten over the shock. "After all, he's catching."

"Oh, I'm not worried about that," she said. "I had the chicken pox in second grade."

"I don't think Ron wants to see anyone, Jamie. After all, he looks a mess right now."

"Well, ask him, will you, Minnie?" she said, her voice getting all soupy. How was I to know that underneath that normal exterior there lurked a Florence Nightingale just waiting for a disease to nurse? "Poor, poor Ron."

Yeck.

"Sure, Jamie," I said. "I'll ask him. But I have to hang up now. Mom just came in."

"Minnie," Mom said, looking even gloomier. "I just found your medical card in the desk, and I'm afraid you didn't have the chicken pox either."

"WHAT!" I screeched. "Oh, cruel fate!"

I staggered out of the kitchen and went up to my room. I threw myself on the bed and spent some time beating my fists and feet into the quilt. Sometimes that helps a person calm down.

After about five minutes I looked over at my gerbils.

"Did you hear that?" I asked George the gerbil. "Me? The chicken pox?"

George didn't say anything, but he's a gerbil of few words. So I put the problem to Georgina. But she was buried under a pile of shreds and wouldn't come out. That's the trouble with gerbils. They're never there when you need them.

I wished I had a dog. Someone who would slobber all over me when I came home. Someone who would lie at my feet, someone who would look happy when I was happy and look sad when I was sad. Gerbils just chew on cardboard, no matter what's going on.

Not only was I about to come down with chicken pox, but from the sound of it, Jamie was about to nurse Ron back to health. I hoped she didn't do anything dumb like start going steady with him again. And not only that, there was nothing for dinner.

Things were looking truly grim.

Chapter 4

SO YOU CAN see what a bad day it was, and the week that followed wasn't much better.

Oh, I didn't come down with the chicken pox. But that didn't mean I wasn't going to. I looked it up in my hygiene book, which said the incubation period was fourteen days. It had only been seven days. I wasn't safe yet.

I also looked up bubonic plague and smallpox, just in case. I was expecting the worst.

Not only that, remember when Georgina wouldn't come out of her shreds? No. She didn't have the chicken pox. She had babies! Now instead of two gerbils, I had eleven gerbils. My mom was not happy, let me tell you. George didn't look too happy either.

And here's the worst part of all: Jamie and Ron got back together again!

I couldn't believe it! Ron didn't even feel that sick. But every time Jamie called up to say she was coming over, Ron would start racing around. He would turn off the TV, hide all his magazines and soda cans under the bed, and pull the shades. Then he'd get into bed, sprawling himself out like a broken machine, and moan and thrash. By the time Jamie got there you'd think he was doing the deathbed scene from one of those dumb movies.

And Jamie fell for it like a ton of bricks. Even my mother was impressed. After Jamie would leave the kitchen with the cup of soup, or whatever, my mother would get this funny look on her face. Sort of like a cross between a smile and a gas pain. But she never said anything.

I, personally, could think of lots of things to say, but Mom said it would be unfair of me to tell Jamie what Ron was doing before she came over. After all, she said, young love is a beautiful thing.

Yeck.

And another thing. This week at KID-TV has been unreal. I thought if I heard the name Simon Gear one more time, I'd throw up. Every news show Lance did mentioned Simon Gear. We had no news yet as to who he really was, but Lance

29

and Mike read every single article about him in the rock magazines.

They talked about his favorite food, his favorite animals, his favorite colors, whether or not he was planning to marry this actress or that girl singer, who he was seen with last night, how long he had been interested in music, and why he decided to be a rock musician instead of a concert pianist. I felt as if I was related to the guy by the time the concert day rolled around.

But he was still a hunk. Even I, Minnie O'Reilly, ended up being unable to ignore his animal magnetism.

To top it all off, Muffin had been doing her aerobics to his music all week. The music wasn't bad, but the look on her face during the deep knee bends and the leg lifts was enough to make a normal person sick.

Sandra claimed she'd gotten three thousand letters to Simon Gear, but I didn't believe it. I don't think there are three thousand people in all of Wellsburg! Well, I guess that isn't true—after all, we have a population of fifty thousand—but how many of them could be teenagers?

Maybe there were old people, like twenty-five-year-olds, who were writing him letters too. Can you picture it? Maybe even some grandmothers! Oh, well.

Sandra read some of the letters on the air. Others, Sandra said, were not fit for the public. What's that supposed to mean? Not grammatical?

Billy had a Simon Gear joke on the weather report every day. At least that's what Billy called them. He would say, for example,

"Well, folks, it's going to be hot and humid—just like the concert is going to be! Be sure and get your tickets for a hot time in the old town tonight, and get in gear for Gear!"

Despite the dumb jokes, Billy isn't too bad—even if his uncle is R. Z. Wells. The good part about Billy is that he's also twelve. That means he hasn't taken the fatal plunge into teenagehood. There's a lot to be said for that.

The most interesting part of the whole week was that even though we'd asked people to call in with information about Simon Gear, not one person knew one thing about him—except what you read in the rock magazines. It's hard to believe that someone who was born and raised in a small city like Wellsburg could escape everyone's notice that way. He must have had plastic surgery and changed his name.

Willow was out every day taping person-in-the-street interviews. She asked at least a hundred people what they knew about Simon Gear. Nothing, is what she'd found out. Absolutely nothing.

What was the hardest part of all, though, was that Lennie never came back. Poor Willow had to do the whole thing with the portable camera pack. I guess Lennie's feelings were really hurt.

But what I wanted to know was, if Lennie was such a tough guy, how could a half-wit like Dave Madison get him upset like that? I certainly didn't believe all that mush I'd said to Willow. I only said it to make her feel as if I was sympathetic to her problem.

I was hoping he'd come back soon. We really needed the van—especially with the concert coming up. We had to be at the bus station to meet Simon Gear's tour bus. That meant we had to have all the equipment, we had to have the entire staff, and Rock Video had to be ready to use his camera to make the video. If we'd had the van, it would have been easy. This way, we were going to look like a high school bicycle tournament.

And we had to get tons of footage, because Dave Madison had sold a lot of ads. I hated to admit it, but he was right about looking dumb if we didn't get the videos. Not only would Dave look dumb, the whole KID-TV staff would look dumb. We'd been promising everyone two great videos, plus concert coverage, plus the moon. At least Jeannie was back. Her impetigo got better. I hadn't caught that, yet, either.

ROCK VIDEO STRIKES AGAIN

Horace, alias Rock, had been calling Simon Gear's manager for a whole week—every half hour—trying to get a commitment to make the video with us. He hadn't gotten any answers at all. But he had overheard what time the bus was arriving—and where. We'd kept this information top secret. Nobody, not even the other TV stations, knew about it. This was going to be our scoop!

Jamie yelled, "Okay everybody. Let's get this show on the road!"

We looked like a crazy camel caravan. Rock Video had his video camera, so Billy and Mike had to carry the two filter thingies. They looked like big white umbrellas, and it was windy out. I figured that Billy and Mike would soon be in the next state with those two things attached to their bikes.

Muffin was crabbing about riding her bike all the way downtown. She'd tried to get her boyfriend, Bruce, to come and drive her. Bruce was a "college man," and he had a brand new red Mustang. But Bruce had football practice and he couldn't come. I was surprised, since Muffin claimed to be in such good shape from doing aerobics all the time. Maybe she just wanted everyone to see Bruce's new car—with her in it.

We finally got organized and moving. We'd allowed an hour to get to the bus depot. It only took us half an hour. It was cold out, and I figured it would probably rain on us all too. But so far, the weather was holding.

When we got there, we set up everything, got the cameras ready and loaded, staked out the entire block, and waited.

Muffin was so excited, she kept going into the ladies' room in the station to fix her hair. Jamie kept breathing deep sighs, and the only one who even began to act at all normal was Kathy Nelligan.

I say normal, because she did what she always did. She ran in place. She looked like she was warming up for baseball.

Billy and I went inside for a hot chocolate. They make their kind with the boiling water and the little pack of powdered chemicals. I love it, but it's always too hot to drink for about twenty minutes. I was blowing on my drink when I heard screaming from outside.

"That sounds like Muffin," Billy said. "I guess Simon Gear has arrived."

Chapter 5

IT WAS SIMON Gear all right, and even I, Minnie O'Reilly, was impressed. The tour bus looked like it was practically a block long. It had those neat windows they have in limousines. You know, the kind that are smoke-colored so you can't see through them.

I would've loved to go inside and see what it looked like, but by the time Billy and I got out there, there was already a giant fight going on.

Simon Gear was standing outside the door of the bus with a strange look on his face. Sort of a combination of horror, anger, and surprise.

This other guy—his manager, obviously—was standing next to him. The other guy was really old—like forty. He had long hair, a flowered shirt, and droopy jeans, and he was smoking a big fat cigar. He wasn't really smoking it, since it wasn't lit. He was more like chewing on it.

Simon Gear was yelling. "So where is everybody?"

Whaddaya mean "everybody"? The whole KID-TV staff was there. What did he expect? Yankee Stadium?

Anyway, he kept right on yelling. "I thought this was supposed to be a real bash! Where are the fans? Where are the promoters? And where are we, anyway? This doesn't look like Wellsburg to me!"

The old guy was saying, "Now, Simon, don't get excited. . . . Trust me. . . . Everything's under control. . . . The cat is in the bag. . . . The promoters will be here any minute. I talked to them just yesterday. And I'm sure there'll be a camera crew. I've been talking to somebody on one of the local stations—KID-TV."

"Yo, man, we're here!" Rock Video said, but nobody paid any attention to him.

"What kind of a [blip blip] manager are you, anyway!" Simon Gear yelled. "If this is Wellsburg, then I'm a short-order cook!"

Jamie sparked into action when she heard that one a second time. She rushed up to Simon Gear and his manager.

"Mr. Gear, welcome to Wellsburg!" she shouted. But Simon Gear turned his back on her and continued to yell at his manager. The guy started chewing his dead cigar even faster than before.

"Now, keep your socks up, Simon," the manager said. "I know you're overtired, and you—"

"Don't tell me I'm overtired, you half-baked excuse for a manager," Simon yelled back. "You're the one who arranged this tour, and I'm the one who's been on the bus for fourteen hours. Where is everybody?"

"Right here!" yelled Jamie as loud as she could, tugging at Simon Gear's arm. "And we have the entire KID-TV staff ready, to make sure your arrival in your hometown is covered totally and com—"

But just then someone from Simon Gear's entourage came out of the bus depot and whispered something in Simon's ear.

I thought I had seen mad until I saw what happened next. I know that when you have to sing in a big stadium to thousands of people, you develop a powerful voice. But I hadn't guessed *how* powerful!

I gathered that what the guy whispered was that the equipment for the concert—you know, the mikes, the booms, the amplifiers and all the costumes, electric pianos, guitars, and drums—nothing important, really—hadn't arrived at the bus depot. They'd had that stuff shipped direct and they were supposed to pick it up and take it over to the stadium.

Well, Simon Gear hit the roof.

"[Blip blip] it, you sleazy windbag," he yelled at the guy with the cigar. "Not only do you mess up my weekend, but you lose all my equipment and send me to the wrong town on top of it all!"

"This isn't the wrong town!" Jamie said, trying to get their attention again. "This is indeed Wellsburg. THE Wellsburg! YOUR Wellsburg, Mr. Gear!"

But no one listened.

"The equipment will get here, Simon baby," the manager was saying in a soothing tone of voice. He probably would have patted Simon Gear on the head, except he was afraid of getting punched. I would have been afraid of getting punched if I were him. "I can promise you, Simon baby—if the equipment doesn't get here, then my name is meatballs."

It went on like this for about fifteen minutes. Simon Gear yelled, the manager said some gobble-dygook, Jamie tried to get a word in, and Simon Gear turned his back on her and yelled some more. And Rock Video was getting it all on videotape. Not exactly an interview, but pretty interesting stuff.

That's when another guy came over to Simon Gear and tapped him on the shoulder. I didn't hear what he said, but it didn't matter. Simon Gear turned beet red.

"Did you hear that!" he screamed at the manager. The guy backed up about two feet. "Did you hear that? Chick here just spoke to the REA man, and guess what, birdbrain? The stuff was shipped last week, and if it isn't in the bus station now, it isn't going to be. He has the [blip blip] receipt that says someone signed for it in Wellsburg! That means it was delivered. But Chick here has been through every box and package in that storeroom, and the [blip blip] equipment isn't there!"

"Now, Simon," the manager said. "There's no sense getting yourself all tiddlywinks about this."

"Tiddlywinks? Tiddlywinks?" Simon Gear screamed. His voice sure could carry. I didn't see why he wanted the amplifiers. It didn't seem to me that he'd need them. "This isn't a kindergarten class, Herman. This is a rock group! Find my equipment, and find it NOW!"

That's when Dave Madison decided to join the fight. He marched right up to them, puffing out his chest in his silly madras jacket. "Mr. Gear, sir. It occurs to me that your equipment was probably sent on to the Wells Memorial Stadium. If you'll just allow me, I'll make a quick call . . ."

"Do that, sonny," Simon Gear said. Then he

turned his back to Dave and went on yelling at the
manager. It was starting to get pretty funny.

The manager kept saying none of it was his
fault, and besides nothing was wrong. Simon Gear
kept saying everything was wrong, and it was all
the manager's fault.

That's when Dave came back with the good news.
The equipment wasn't at the stadium, either.

Well, everyone went crazy. Simon Gear was yelling, the manager was yelling, all the other musi-
cians and stage hands and lighting guys were
yelling. The bus driver started yelling too.

"Where are the costumes?"

"Where are the [blip blip] promoters?"

"Who's in charge here?"

"I'm not moving from this spot until I find out
where my drums are."

"I'm not moving from this spot until I find out
where the [blip] I'm supposed to be going!"

"Where are we, anyway? This doesn't look like
Wellsburg to me!"

"If I don't get some sleep, I'll go crazy!"

"If I don't get some food, I'll go crazy!"

"I'm already crazy. Let's go back to New York!"

Then Simon Gear turned on us—probably because we were the only ones he hadn't really yelled
at yet.

He started out real quiet. "Tell me, miss. What

town is this?" he said to Jamie. "This doesn't look anything like my hometown."

"This is it, Mr. Gear," Jamie said, happy to have his attention at last. "Everything is ready, the fans have their tickets, and the Wells Memorial Stadium is just waiting for the concert tonight. And we'd like to get an exclusive interview with you. How does it feel to finally be back after all this . . ."

Simon Gear slowly looked around him. He looked at the tree-lined street, the buildings, the public library, the town hall, and the VFW post headquarters. Then he turned his back on Jamie again.

"Herman," he said quietly. "Herman, I don't know what you did, but this isn't my hometown. This may be *a* Wellsburg, but it isn't the Wellsburg I was born in. I want to know where the [blip] I am, Herman. I'm about to give a homecoming concert without any instruments or equipment in a place I've never been in before in my life."

Chapter 6

I COULDN'T BELIEVE it! I, Minnie O'Reilly, had personally heard on TV that Simon Gear was from Wellsburg. And not just on KID-TV, either. After all, when Simon Gear does a homecoming concert, they talk about it in other places, too—like channel four and channel two!

What did he mean, he'd never been here before in his life? How could he have never been here in his life if he was born here?

For a minute I didn't know where *I* was either. There was dead silence on the sidewalk. Simon Gear didn't say anything, his group didn't say anything, his staff didn't say anything. Only Herman the manager was talking.

"Listen Simon baby. You told me you were born in Wellsburg, so I booked a concert for Wellsburg.

42

What can I say? So it's the wrong Wellsburg? So what! So we'll give the concert anyway! We'll make some money, and then we'll go home. Not a bad idea, right?"

"Wrong, Herman," Simon snarled. "It's a bad idea for a couple of reasons. For one thing, how were you planning to give this concert, I ask you? It doesn't matter which Wellsburg we're in. We have no equipment. We have no costumes. We have no instruments! I presume you're going to tell me that's not your fault either?"

As Simon Gear ran all this through, his voice got higher and louder. His face got redder and madder.

"Listen, you half-baked, tone-deaf gorilla!" he continued while Herman was babbling about making money, and what difference did it make, and how the stuff was going to arrive any minute now—trust him—and how he would make it up to him next time, "I can't remember how I ended up with you as my manager, but YOU'RE FIRED!"

Herman went right on babbling. "Now, Simon. You know how you get when you're about to go on stage. And I understand completely. . . . I won't hold this against you, believe me."

Simon Gear wasn't getting any calmer.

A big Trailways bus wheezed around the corner and pulled to a stop behind the tour bus. The door hissed open, and two women with blue hair and flowered silk dresses climbed down the steps. Then the driver climbed out behind them. He opened the big side door on the bus and took out two canvas suitcases, three shopping bags, and a birdcage with a cover on it.

"Itchy kitchy koo," the taller woman said to the birdcage as they picked up their things. For a minute they stared at the whole entourage on the sidewalk. Then they prissed up their lips, stuck their noses in the air, and staggered off with their stuff.

That was when Simon Gear took poor Herman by the neck and picked him up. Oh, my goodness, I thought. Simon Gear is about to murder his manager right before our innocent little eyes!

But instead, he put him on the bottom step of the Trailways bus and gave him a shove. Herman toppled into the bus like a duffel bag full of old boots. The bus driver looked surprised, but Simon Gear smiled at him sweetly and reached into his pocket. "Here's a hundred dollars," he said. "Take this dumbbell to wherever it is you're going . . . and keep the change."

The door hissed shut, and the big Trailways pulled away from the curb. I could see Herman the manager's nose pressed up against the window. His cigar had gotten mashed flat. I only hoped that Willow or Rock had gotten the whole sequence

44

on tape. I wondered how much one of the big networks would pay for a scene like that. It was a historic event.

We all were suddenly very quiet as we watched the Trailways bus get smaller and smaller.

I knew why we were quiet. We were waiting to see what was going to happen next. I guess that was going through the minds of the group with Simon Gear too. It was obvious no one knew what to do now that there was no manager.

"Oh, mashed potatoes!" Willow snapped. Willow sometimes says something really strange like "mashed potatoes" or "ant hills" when she'd really rather swear.

"What's wrong?" asked Jamie.

"I just ran out of tape," Willow said.

"It doesn't matter," Jamie said, patting Willow on the back. "After all, nothing's happening anymore anyway. Did you get that stuff with the manager, at least?"

"It's all right here," Willow said with a half smile. "But it isn't exactly the rip-roaring welcome party we thought it would be. Some homecoming!"

That's when Simon Gear threw his hands up in the air and started pacing back and forth in front of the door of the tour bus. Everyone else just watched him. It almost looked as if they were

45

afraid of him, and I can understand why: the look on his face was the look bad guys in the movies get when they're about to push someone's face in. I guess the people in his group knew enough to stay away from him when he got that look.

Not so Dave Madison. He wasn't the world's most sensitive human being, but of course you already know that. It was just hard to believe that even Dave Madison could be standing there, beaming away like a Christmas tree. I wondered what he had up his sleeve.

"Hey, Jamie," whispered Rock Video, "I'm going to interview the other members of the group. I'll get candid interviews with them as individuals. We can splice that stuff in with the concert tapes. It'll make for great material!"

Jamie stood and nodded. "Great idea, Rock," she said softly. And then Rock walked away from the KID-TV group and started to slither across the sidewalk. He looked like a cat sneaking up on a bird. He tapped a guy with long blond hair that looked as if it had come off a hay wagon. The guy was wearing a leather vest with studs all over it, and no shirt. I wondered if he was cold, as I waited to find out what Dave was up to.

I didn't have to wait long. Dave launched himself out of the crowd and put his hand on Simon Gear's shoulder. "Simon, my friend," he said in this oily phony-friendly voice he gets when he's about to sell someone something. "I can see that you could use a little help. I want to make it clear that I'm offering you my services as manager in the . . . er . . . absence of Mr. . . . er . . . Herman. I know this town like the back of my hand. I know the entertainment business even better. As the business manager of a TV station, I feel I can . . ."

Simon Gear shook Dave's hand off his shoulder and started to climb into the bus. Everyone watched, dumbfounded.

Everyone, that is, except Muffin. Muffin raced across the sidewalk just as Simon Gear disappeared into the bus. Dave Madison was right behind Simon Gear, and Muffin was right behind Dave. Dave was jabbering away about all his great qualities, when Muffin caught up with him.

As Simon Gear disappeared into the bus, Dave had his foot on the bottom step. That's when Muffin grabbed a handful of his madras jacket. She pulled him right off the bottom step and threw him out of the way. He bounced off the side of the bus and fell flat on his rear end. While he was getting his wits back, Muffin climbed up after Simon Gear.

She was saying "I'll be your secretary, your gofer, your anything. I've had experience as . . ."

She disappeared into the bus. Dave picked himself up and climbed in after her. Both of them were talking a mile a minute.

What a break, I thought. We get rid of two of the worst pains on the station. But poor Simon. Next thing he knew, he'd be doing commercial spots for Zitzoff's Miracle Pimple Cream.

Lance ran to the door. "Hey, Dave," he yelled. "I don't remember hearing you'd quit! I thought you had to give two weeks . . ."

Rock Video pushed past Lance right then, rushing from his interview with the drummer to get inside coverage of Simon Gear hiring Dave and Muffin as road manager and secretary.

He got in the doorway just in time to get hit full in the chest with Dave Madison.

Rock Video fell over backward, and his video camera flew out of his hand. It landed about six feet away, right on its lens. There was a nasty sound—the sound of a lens breaking.

Dave howled. Rock Video howled louder. But both howls were nothing compared with the howl that came next: the howl of Muffin Prendergast as she too came out the door of the bus.

Unfortunately, Muffin came out walking. I would have preferred to see her come out flying too. I guess Simon Gear is a gentleman. Maybe his mother told him, no matter how pesky a girl is, no matter how pushy and stupid, you still can't throw her out of any open doors or windows. Too bad.

But that wasn't the worst thing. The worst thing was that Rock hadn't been able to tape the best scene of all. If he hadn't been in such a rush to get into the bus, we would have a tape of the grand exits of Dave and Muffin to watch over and over again until we were old and feeble.

I began to wish I had the chicken pox.

Chapter 7

DAVE AND MUFFIN didn't see the humor in what had happened, but everyone else did. Dave was dusting himself off, Muffin punched him in the arm—hard.

"What's the matter with you?" Dave squeaked.

"You ruined everything, you half-wit!" she snapped. Then she stuck her nose in the air and marched into the bus station. I guess she went to powder her nose—isn't that what you do when it's out of joint?

Dave twitched his shoulders and said, "He said he'd give me a ring when they check into the hotel."

"Don't call me, I'll call you—eh, Dave?" I said.

Dave scowled at me, and then he went into the bus station too. I guess he wanted to powder *his* nose.

One by one, all the Simon Gear roadies got onto the bus, and the door hissed shut. We all stood there, waiting for something to happen.

Jamie tapped my arm. "Minnie, what are we going to do?" she wailed. "We promised full coverage and an exclusive interview. All we have is a lot of screaming and yelling. We promised something we can't deliver! I feel awful!"

"Don't feel awful," I said. "After all, we can get an interview later."

"It won't be as easy as you think," Jamie said. "Did you see how that Simon Gear treats us? He wouldn't give us the time of day! What makes you think we'll *ever* get an interview?"

"Don't worry, Jamie," I said, trying to think fast. "I'll handle that part. You just get the rest of the staff organized. I'll figure out a way to get Simon Gear to give us what we want."

"I don't see how you're going to do it," Jamie said.

"I, Minnie O'Reilly, never fail! Neither snow, nor rain, nor heat, nor gloom of night . . ."

"That's the mailman, Minnie," Billy said.

"That's me, too, Billy," I said, trying to sound as if I knew what I was doing.

I was hoping something would come to me. It usually does, but I can't always count on it to come to me exactly when I need it. Sometimes it comes to me the next day. The next day wasn't good enough this time.

"I could use some more tape," Willow said.

"Do I have to go on the air with just this little bit of material?" Lance whined. "How am I going to do a news show with this garbage?"

"The same way you always do," I said. "Fake it."

"What about my lens?" Rock wailed.

"Do you have any more at home?" Jamie asked, concerned.

"Yes," he said, looking glum. "But they aren't good ones."

"A crummy lens is better than no lens," said Mike McGee. "I'll go back with Lance, Jamie. I'll write the broadcast for him. We only need Jeannie to be on camera, anyway, so it can be a sort of interrupted broadcast."

The reason the broadcast would be interrupted was that it was Saturday. Usually we didn't have any shows on Saturday. Saturdays were devoted to educational programs, like those movies about the Grand Canyon that were made in the 1950s. Mr. Hurley put them all on a continuous tape, and then he sat back and marked papers.

Mr. Hurley was the head of the Biology Department, and he taught a lot of classes too. He also gave a lot of tests. I hoped I didn't get Mr. Hurley for biology when I got into high school. I heard he was tough . . . and boring. That's a terrible combination.

So Rock Video got on his bike and headed home for his extra lenses. Lance and Mike and Jeannie got on their bikes and headed for the studio.

The rest of us just stood around. As I was trying to figure out how to get an interview with a really grouchy rock star, and Jamie was trying to figure out what to do next, the tour bus was just sitting there. I guessed they were all inside doing the same thing.

The door hissed open, and the guy with the straw hair poked his head out. "Is there a decent hotel in this burg?" he said to Jamie.

"Of course! the Wellsburg Arms," Jamie answered.

"And where is this paradise on earth located?" he asked.

"At the corner of Fifth and Maple," yelled Dave. He'd just come out of the bus station. "I'll ride over there with you, and make sure the accommodations are good enough for your . . ."

Before he could finish the sentence, the door hissed shut.

"Well, don't bother to thank me!" Jamie yelled at the door.

She was mad.

The door hissed open again, and the yellow head popped out for a second, "Thanks, sweetheart," the guy said with a grin. "Now, let me give you some advice. Don't take any wooden nickels . . . especially from that kid in the madras jacket!"

The bus drove off.

"Follow that bus!" I yelled. "Come on, men!" I hopped on my bike. Billy was right behind me.

Jamie and Willow stared at me for a second, and then they hopped on their bikes too.

"We have no tape," yelled Willow.

"Don't worry," I yelled back. "There's a camera shop on the way! You can always buy some, and we'll pay you back later!"

"I'm the one who should make those decisions!" howled Dave. He looked funny, with his jacket and tie flying out behind him as he pedaled along furiously trying to catch up with Jamie.

"Wait for me!" screeched Muffin. She'd just come out of the station. "Where's everybody going? Where's Simon? What's happeninnnnggg?"

Nobody answered. We had a bus to catch.

Well. You guessed it. The bus got there ahead of us, and by the time Willow got the tape and Dave got his act together about the receipts and everything, we missed the part where they all checked into the hotel.

There was anothing but a big empty bus in the back parking lot.

And there was nothing but a big, nasty doorman in front of the hotel. Even after Jamie explained that we were the press here to cover Simon Gear's arrival and concert, he still wouldn't let us in. He wouldn't even let us into the lobby! It was outrageous.

Dave said he was going to call the manager and have the doorman fired, but the doorman laughed at him. Willow got some really great footage of the doorman yelling at us, however.

"Maybe we'd better try something else," Jamie finally said. "This guy won't let us put one foot in the lobby, much less go up to Simon Gear's suite."

"We could stand around here until he comes out again," said Muffin. She had stars in her eyes, and her makeup was on differently. She had frowzed up her hair so it looked like she'd kept it under the sink for a week, and she'd painted a big red mouth on top of where her little skinny one was usually found.

"That's no good," said Willow. "We have to try and get an appointment for an interview. To do that, we have to make sure he knows we're here."

"Which reminds me," I said. "We have to let Lance and Mike and Jeannie know we're at the hotel. And Rock Video too. They think we're still at the bus station, remember?"

"How're we going to do that?" asked Muffin. Sometimes her dumbness surprises even me.

"We're going to use the te-le-phone," I said. "Have you heard about those? People use them to speak to other people who aren't in the same general area. That's why they invented them."

"Good thought, Minnie," said Jamie. "I'd forgotten all about Rock. He, especially, needs to know where we are. Would you please give him a ring?"

But that was easier said than done. Actually, the germ of an idea had begun to form in my busy little brain. I'd decided that it was a perfect opportunity to get myself into the hotel lobby.

All I had to do was tell the big, ugly doorman that I needed to use the phone, and then once inside . . . all I had to do was scoot up the back stairs . . . find a chambermaid or something . . . and get the number of Simon Gear's suite. After that, it would be a cinch to get him to agree to an interview.

Unfortunately, things didn't work out exactly that way. When I told the doorman I had to use the telephone, he told me I had to use the one on the corner.

So much for plan A. I was now down to plan B. But what exactly was plan B?

I found two quarters, called Rock, and then the studio. Of course I didn't get any of the kids. I got Mr. Hurley.

It was while I was trying to explain things to Mr. Hurley that I got an itch on my shoulder. I was scratching it while I was giving him the message. Then I realized what I was doing.

"Oh, no!" I yelled into the phone. "The pox!"

Chapter 8

OF COURSE, MR. Hurley got upset when he heard me scream "The pox!" You see, he thought I meant the bubonic plague. But that's another whole story.

I wasn't even thinking about Mr. Hurley when I hung up, so you can imagine how surprised I was later on when I heard the Board of Health had come to visit my parents, when I wasn't there to explain the problem.

Fortunately my dad took care of it. It took them a while to get it straightened out that I was talking about the chicken pox. Mr. Hurley must have thrown quite a scare into whoever he called up to report the end of the world as we know it. Dad even had to take the guy up to Ron's room and give him the name of Dr. Ferguson. Good old Dad always manages to keep a cool head in times of crisis.

Anyway, after I hung up on Mr. Hurley, I went screaming back out of the phone booth about having the pox. Everyone out there backed away from me. Can you believe it? Let me tell you, that is not a great feeling.

Everyone but Jamie of course. She figured it out in half a second. I suppose it didn't hurt that she knew about Ron, but you see what I mean about her being smart. Not for one minute did she think I meant the bubonic plague.

"Jamie," I said sadly. "Look, I can't hang around a great star like Simon Gear when I'm contagious. I have to leave."

"I really don't see why, Minnie," Jamie said. "After all, most people had the chicken pox in the second grade. You should only leave if you feel too sick to help."

"I don't feel even the littlest bit sick," I snapped. "And even if I did, I wouldn't care! The show must go on!"

"Then why not stay?" said Jamie.

"I can't," I wailed. "Besides, how can you be *sure* Simon Gear already had the chicken pox? After all, if I can get it, and Ron can get it, then it is almost a sure bet that Simon Gear can get it too. No. I must be strong. I have to be selfless in this case. A *real* heroine wouldn't dream of ending the career of a great man like Simon Gear. I have to leave and not see him . . . ever! Or anyone else for the next two weeks!"

"Hey, Minnie." It was Billy, standing next to me. "I had the chicken pox in second grade. I don't have to worry about being around you."

"Oh, Billy," I said. And I know this sounds mushy, but I was really glad that Billy wasn't scared of me. I really needed a friend. Having him say that helped me pull myself together.

"Actually," I said, feeling tons better already, "I have an idea. Billy and I can do a lot more good away from the hotel."

Jamie looked puzzled.

"We can locate the equipment," I said. "After all, what better way to get Simon Gear's attention than to be in possession of his instruments and amplifiers. I bet he'd be really glad to talk to us then, right?"

"You're absolutely right!" Jamie squealed, clapping her hands together.

Even Dave was impressed. "Good thinking, Minnie," he said. Then he said, "It's going to be like blackmail! When we get the stuff, all we do is say 'Simon baby, if you want the goods, you'd better talk!' "

"Dave, that is *not* the way we're going to handle it," I said. "You really are a class A, number one sleaze. Did you know that?"

He didn't seem to care.

Billy and I got on our bikes and headed for my house. At least we could get some food, and we could start trying to figure out what happened to the shipment.

Five peanut butter sandwiches and four glasses of milk later, we knew nothing.

"I've looked through every one of these stupid rock magazines," I finally said after swallowing a mouthful of peanut butter, "and they all say the same thing! Simon Gear is from Wellsburg!"

"Then why did he say he's never seen this place?" Billy asked. "And how does that help us?"

"I don't know," I said. "And to answer your second question, I don't know that either. After all, how many Wellsburgs could there be?"

Billy looked gloomy.

But as soon as I heard myself say "How many Wellsburgs could there be? " I had a thought.

I, Minnie O'Reilly, was personally about to solve this case! I almost choked on the peanut butter I'd just put in my mouth.

Which is something else that has always bothered me. How can they keep saying that peanut butter sticks to your ribs? I have yet to get the peanut butter off the roof of my mouth!

"That's it!" I yelled, when I finally got it swallowed. "I bet the equipment got shipped to another Wellsburg by accident. Even better, I bet this other Wellsburg is the *right* Wellsburg!"

"What do you mean the 'right' Wellsburg?" Billy asked. It was obvious that I wasn't making myself clear. Maybe the fever had begun to affect my brain. I tried again.

"I bet that there's another Wellsburg, and I bet *that's* the Wellsburg that Simon Gear came from. His equipment probably got shipped to the 'right' place, and the concert was probably arranged in the other Wellsburg."

"Which other Wellsburg?" said Billy, puzzled. Sometimes he's quick, and sometimes he's not.

"Our Wellsburg is the other Wellsburg," I said.

"How many Wellsburgs could there be?"

Didn't I just say that? Maybe it was déjà vu.

"For all I know, there could be hundreds . . . thousands!" I said, running to the bookcase. "We'll start by looking up all the Wellsburgs in the almanac!"

Which is exactly what we did.

And that's exactly what we found.

There was at least one Wellsburg in every state of the union. Sometimes three or four of them, counting places with names like Wellsburg Landing, Wellsburg Junction, and Wellsburg in the Dale. That sort of thing really makes a person feel unique, let me tell you.

"It's a wonder we ever get any junk mail at all," Billy said, his voice full of wonder.

"Cheer up," I said. "Maybe we only get half of it."

But this was no time for jokes. We only had a little while to figure out which Wellsburg bus station held the equipment. This would take a lot of telephoning . . . and a lot of money too.

I could just picture what my mom and dad would do when they got the phone bill for this one!

I, personally, didn't want to risk it.

I was sitting there trying to figure out a way to make four thousand phone calls when Ron appeared in the doorway. He was wearing this really dumb pair of pajamas . . . you know, the kind with horses heads all over them. When he saw Billy, he started to run back upstairs.

"Don't get excited," I yelled after him. "It's only Billy and me. Jamie is at a hotel with Simon Gear!"

Ron came slouching back in. "I needed to get a soda," he said. "And a sandwich or something. Is there any pizza in this house?"

He didn't even care where Jamie was! All he cared about was whether she was going to catch him eating and not moaning. Oh, well.

"And what are you two guys doing inside on

such a gorgeous day?" he said. "Shouldn't you be out in the sandbox or something?"

Billy doesn't have any brothers or sisters, so he didn't get the insult.

"Oh, Ron," he said. "We have to make about a thousand phone calls, and we don't know what to do about the money."

"Steal a credit card," Ron said, as he opened the refrigerator door and looked in.

"From who?" I asked. "Nobody around here even knows the kind of people who have a credit card you use in a telephone. What kind of a family do you think this is?"

Ron just grunted. He was loading stuff up to take back to bed with him. I shuddered at the thought of what his room must smell like by now. I knew for a fact that whenever Jamie came he shoved whatever he'd been stuffing his face with under the bed. I'm positive he never took any of it out when she left.

He had a loaf of bread, a jar of anchovy paste, three cans of soda, two bananas, and a dish of left-over applesauce. I could see there were going to be wildlife management problems upstairs before this illness was through.

"Actually," Billy said after a while, "I know someone who has a credit card. But we can't steal it."

"Why not?" Ron said.

" 'Cause it's Uncle Rufus, that's why," Billy said.

And that's when I knew our troubles were over. Of course! Why hadn't I thought of it before? We just had to make Uncle Rufus let us use his telephone. Not only could he afford it, but he might have some reason to want to make sure the concert came off.

I had just that very second recalled something about good ol' Uncle Rufus owning all the concession stands in the Wells Memorial Stadium. If there was no equipment, there would be no concert. If there was no concert, no one would buy hot dogs. If no one bought hot dogs, Uncle Rufus wouldn't get his percentage.

"Let's go," I said to Billy. "And let's bring the almanac too."

We got to the Wells mansion in about four minutes, but old Rufus the Doofus wasn't around. Fritz the butler said he thought Mr. Wells was at his office downtown.

I scratched my shoulder a few more times, and then off we went. I was getting far too much exercise for a deathly sick person, but anything for the cause, I thought.

Ten minutes later we saw the limousine parked out in front. We were in luck. One minute later we were riding up in the elevator in the Wells Building. We went all the way to the top—right into the lair of R. Z. himself.

Chapter 9

THE DOORS WHOOSHED open on the fifteenth floor, and Billy and I stepped out of the elevator onto the nice, squishy carpeting. Since it was Saturday, Miss McGillicuddy—Rufus the Doofus's watchdog-secretary combination—wasn't sitting at her desk.

That was good, because my experience with Miss McGillicuddy hasn't been all that positive in the past. She's not an easy lady to get around. I guess that's why old R. Z. hired her.

I looked at all those comfy-looking pale brown leather chairs, wishing I could just flop down in one. But no. We had a mission! Billy went over and knocked on the big carved-oak doors that led into the inner sanctum.

"Now what?" came a crabby voice from the other side. The door was flung open, and Billy almost

66

fell forward into Uncle Rufus's arms. "Great jumping Jehoshaphat, boy! What are you doing here?"

"I just . . ." Billy began. But Uncle Rufus didn't let Billy finish his sentence. He never let anyone finish sentences. I guess he thought of it as one of his trademarks.

"So-o-o-o-o . . . I see you brought that nasty little girl with you," he said, looking right at me.

I was insulted. I am *not* little. I am only short.

"And a good thing, too, kids," he said with a horrible sort of smile on his face. "You came just in time to see a special broadcast from my very own KID-TV. I believe you two have something to do with this slop, right?"

Billy's Uncle Rufus thought the KID-TV as "his" television station because he provided some of the funding to get it started. He was really using the station to get himself some good publicity. And take it from me, he really needed it. Most of what he got was terrible. But all he ever did was complain about how awful we were, and how he was going to close us down. He's a real sweet guy.

R.Z. walked across the thick carpeting sort of like a crab moving sideways. He turned up the volume on his television set, and then sat down behind his humungous desk. There was Lance, grinning out of the box like an idiot.

"Well, all you Simon Gear fans," Lance was

67

saying. "Here's the beginning of our exclusive coverage of the great, the stupendous Simon Gear Homecoming Concert."

Then the screen switched from Lance to the tape Willow and Rock got outside the bus station. While the tape ran, Lance talked in a voice-over: "Yessir, fans, KID-TV was there when the Simon Gear tour bus pulled into the Wellsburg bus depot. As you can see, Simon Gear stepped out of the bus and was overwhelmed to be back in his hometown."

Here's what we saw: Simon Gear climbing out of the tour bus with a strange look on his face—like he'd landed on the moon by accident. Then Herman the manager right behind him, chewing on his cigar. Then Simon shaking his fist at Herman the manager's face.

And then Lance said, "Yessir, fans. The whole group was there and delighted to be in Wellsburg, finally. While the KID-TV staff made sure that everything was proceeding smoothly, and preparations for the concert were moving along as planned, there was an excited exchange of information. The number of fans expected and the hit songs Simon will sing were just two of the topics covered."

And here's what we saw: Simon Gear's group climbing out of the tour bus, and then standing around as Simon and Herman screamed at each other. There was no sound, of course, but it wasn't hard to tell that the two of them were not happy.

Then Lance said, "After checking to make sure that things were going smoothly for the group, Simon and his staff bid a fond farewell to the familiar Wellsburg bus depot."

Here's what we saw: Simon Gear picking up Herman the manager by the neck and throwing him on the Trailways bus. After he handed the money to the driver, we saw the bus depart. Then we saw Simon Gear yelling at the camera.

Here's what Lance said to wrap it all up: "The KID-TV team is now at the hotel—the famous Wellsburg Arms on Maple and Fifth, where Simon will be staying until after the concert. We'll be bringing you up-to-date coverage all day as this story breaks."

Here's what we saw: Muffin knocking Dave out of the way and climbing up the steps of the bus, and a quick shot of the top of the straw-haired guy's head followed by a whole topsy-turvy piece of tape. It showed the trees, the sky, what looked like Dave's madras elbow, and the side of the bus. Then a great crack spread across the screen, and the tape ended.

I was impressed. Uncle Rufus was not.

"Well, kiddies," he said, "your work is up to par as usual, I see."

I was about to explain to him that we were just beginning, when he interrupted me. I know it hardly seems to be an interruption if you haven't started talking yet, but I was breathing in.

"I don't watch your show too often—only when it's important. And without fail, you kids seem to mess up the important coverage."

"Uncle Rufus . . ." said Billy. "Uncle Rufus, we need your help, because . . ."

"I'll say you need some help," R.Z. said. "More help than anyone on this earth is able to give you, I suspect."

"No, really, Uncle Rufus," Billy said. I hoped he didn't cry or anything. But I wouldn't have blamed him. R.Z. Wells makes you either want to fight or blubber.

"Look, Mr. Wells," I said, standing in front of Billy. "We didn't come up here to watch your TV set. We came up here because there's supposed to be a concert tonight in the Wells Memorial Stadium—but it won't come off unless you let us use your telephone."

"And why not, young lady?" he answered, looking suspicious. "What have you done to mess up the concert?"

"You don't have to look at me like that," I said. and I squinted my eyes up so I'd look as mean as he did. I leaned my elbows on his desk, and got my face real close to his tie clip. "The sound equipment—which includes amplifiers, booms, mikes, and instruments—as well as their costumes, was delivered to the wrong Wellsburg. No equipment, no concert, right?"

I stared at Rufus the Doofus, and he stared at me. He was giving me a look as if he thought I'd managed to personally hide all the stuff, and was about to make a deal with him for its return. If he wanted to look at it that way, that was his business. But he was so weird! Who would think a couple of twelve-year-olds would steal a bunch of musical instruments and then blackmail some totally unrelated person with it? Beats me.

Anyway, I decided that it might actually be the best way to get R.Z. to help. He certainly wouldn't do it out of the goodness of his heart—because he has no heart. If he wanted to think it was blackmail, let him think that. As long as I got to use his telephone.

"What do you want from me?" he said, and his eyes got just as narrow and squinty as mine.

I leaned a little farther forward. "I already told you. I want to use your phone."

R.Z. sat back in his big executive chair and put the tips of his fingers together. He pursed up his livery lips and squinted some more. "What could be the harm in that?" he said.

I almost laughed out loud. He'd find out next month when the telephone bill came in.

"I'll just step outside to Miss McGillicuddy's desk," I said. Then I stood up straight and gave Billy a shove toward the door. "We might be a while, since we have to do some research."

Billy and I quickly backed out the door, and it swung shut in our faces.

Fourteen seconds later, the door swung open again. It was R.Z., and I got worried that he was about to take it all back. But no, we were in luck.

"I'm meeting with a client," he said. "I'll be back later. But if I'm not, when you leave, let the guard downstairs know so he can come and lock the office behind you."

"No problem, sir," I said.

Thank goodness, I thought. If he knew how many calls we were about to make—and to where—he'd have a cow! It'd be better if he didn't find out until later. Much later.

R.Z. left, and we started dialing. Billy used the phone next to one of the chairs, and I used the phone at Miss McGillicuddy's desk. That's the great thing about office phones. They have extensions. I decided to speak to Dad about installing phones like that in our house.

We called Directory Assistance in every state and got the bus depot numbers of every Wellsburg bus station. We must have called one hundred and twelve bus stations.

I thought I was going to be forced to have my ear amputated. It was all swollen and red, like a sore thumb. We were on the phone for two and a half hours, and we had no luck at all!

"We're back to square one," I said to Billy, after I hung up on Wellsburg, Alaska. He had just hung up on Wellsburg, Utah. "Now what?"

"Maybe we missed one," he said. Then he sat back against the wall and closed his eyes. "Just let me think for a minute, okay?"

I knew better than to interrupt him. You see, Billy has this photographic memory. I guessed that what he was doing was mentally checking off every listing in the almanac. I wondered why he bothered, since he had the almanac with us . . . or did we?

Where was it? I couldn't remember bringing it up in the elevator with us. But I remembered leaving the house with it, and putting it under the metal clip on my back fender.

"You keep on thinking, Billy," I said. "I have to check on something."

I ran out of the office and pushed the button for the elevator. I would have taken the stairs, but what the heck. I was supposed to be sick, right? But I want you to know that I, Minnie O'Reilly have gotten down those fifteen flights in fourteen seconds. But that was when I was younger . . . and healthier.

Anyway, when I got outside, I was in for a nasty surprise. No almanac. Just the bikes. I could have kicked myself. The book probably slid out of the clip when I went around the corner at Elm and Third. I always take that corner a little too fast. Now we had no way to double-check.

Not that I didn't trust Billy's memory, you understand. But sometimes it works better to have things in writing, instead of floating around inside of someone's head.

I took the elevator back upstairs with my fingers crossed. When I got inside the office, Billy was still sitting there, looking zonked. Oh, great, I thought. He probably put himself to sleep.

"Hey, Billy," I said, "any luck?"

Then Billy got this smile on his face that was wonderful. But a little weird.

"I've got it!" he said, opening his eyes. "Right before the 'Wellsburg' listing, there was one that was spelled funny. It was spelled W-e-l-l-e-s-b-u-r-g, and I think we should give it a try."

Chapter 10

BY THIS TIME it was coming up on one o'clock in the afternoon. There wasn't too much time left, and I was worried about what we would do if we actually *did* find all this phantom equipment. After all, it was one thing to know where it was. It would be quite another to get it back here to Wellsburg in time for the concert.

I crossed my fingers and said, "Billy, do you happen to have a mental picture of what state it's in?"

"State?" he said, looking a little foggy. He always gets a little foggy after he's been tranced out like that. "Oh, right, I know what you mean. Yeah, it's right in our state."

"Our state," I said. Things could be worse, but our state is big.

So we called Directory Assistance, got the number of the express office in Wellesburg, and gave them a call.

"May I help you?" said a gravelly voice.

"Yes, sir," I said. "You wouldn't happen to have a delivery of musical instruments and amplifiers and trunks and stuff like that, would you?"

"I couldn't say, ma'am," came the voice. "I just came on, and I don't recollect seeing anything that fits that description."

"Could you please look?" I asked. "It's awfully important."

"Hang on a sec," said the voice.

I heard the phone being dropped, and then some shuffling noises. There was scrabbling and phumphing, and more shuffling, and then the voice was back.

"Got a whole load of stuff here for one 'S. Gear.' Izzat what you want? It don't look like instruments to me, though . . . except there's drums in there. The other stuff don't look like it anything much. But there's a lot of it."

It took me a couple of seconds to get my breath. "That's the stuff, sir," I said. It came out awfully squeaky, but who cared. "Now could you tell me exactly where you are?"

There was a long silence. "I am in the express office," he said, finally.

"No, no, no," I said. "I mean, where is this Wellesburg express office."

"Hah, hah," said the man. "I thought that was a pretty weird question. After all, where did you call me? Hah, hah. You're a real comedian, miss."

"Thank you," I said. "Where exactly did you say?"

"Oh, right," he said slowly. "Let's see, we're on the corner of Elm and Sycamore streets in south Wellesburg. That's about twelve miles north of Dickens."

"Dickens?" I said. "Where's that?"

"Funny you don't know," he said.

"I'm not from around here," I said. This was getting stupid. "I mean, where are you in the state? North, south, east, or west?"

"West," said the guy. "Are you coming to get this stuff or what?"

"I don't know," I said. "Is there any way you could ship it out right now? I need it in about five hours at the latest."

"Oh, wow," he said. Things didn't look good. "Five hours?"

"Can you do it?"

"Oh, miss, I'm afraid the next bus out of here isn't leaving until tomorrow morning. We only have one pickup a day out of here. Your best bet would be to come yourself and pick it up. That's the only way you'll get it today."

"Oh, well. Just thought I'd ask. We'll be there this afternoon," I said. I hoped we would, but what the heck. Promise them anything, right? "My name is O'Reilly."

"Got it, Miss O'Reilly," said the voice. "The stuff will be here waiting for you."

He hung up with a chuckle, and I hung up with a groan.

"Billy," I said, "I've got good news and bad news."

"I know the good news," he said. "I'm not deaf. What's the bad news?"

"They can't ship us the equipment today, we have to pick it up."

"So, we'll pick it up."

"How, Billy?" I said. "First of all, it's someplace on the other end of the state. And second of all, were you planning to bring all that junk here on the bikes?"

"Oh. Right," he said. "I forgot about that."

"What we need is a great big car," I said. I looked around the office. "And do you know what? I know someone who has a great big car."

Billy looked around too. He got a thoughtful expression on his face, and pushed his glasses back up his nose. Then he said, "I think I know who you mean, but how were you planning to get him to give it to you?"

"I thought I'd ask," I said.

"How are you going to ask him if he isn't here?" It was a good question, I had to admit. I couldn't think of an answer. That was unusual for me.

We sat there and stared at each other for a while. Then, as if in answer to our silent prayers, the door to the office swung open, and guess who walked in.

That's right, Uncle Rufus.

He looked even meaner than he had earlier. "What in the name of tarnation are you two still doing here?" he said.

"Boy, am I ever glad to see you, sir," I said. Then I smiled up at his mottled face, and batted my eyelashes at him as fast as I could. It was something I'd seen Muffin do. She wouldn't do it if it didn't work, so I figured I'd give it a try.

It seemed to work! Old R.Z. looked almost normal without the frown and the sneer.

"What do you want now?" asked Uncle Rufus. He looked at Billy and then back to me.

"Could we borrow the limousine for the afternoon?" I asked.

"What for?" asked Uncle Rufus.

"To pick up the equipment for the concert tonight," said Billy.

Uncle Rufus looked like he was going to swallow his cigar. His face turned red, and then blue, and

79

then purple. "The concert with that disgusting and revolting Gear person?" he howled.

What was the matter with him? I thought. Of course, it was for Simon Gear! Who did he think was giving the concert? Lawrence Welk?

I was about to ask, when he answered the question.

"I didn't know that disgusting punk was going to give a concert in MY stadium until just a few moments ago. My client told me who was on for tonight . . . and even played some of his disgusting music for me on a tape. Well, I didn't listen for more than two minutes, let me tell you! REVOLTING STUFF!"

"What do you think Simon Gear is doing in Wellsburg?" I asked. "Watching the leaves change color?"

"Don't you talk that way to me, young lady," said Uncle Rufus. "I had *no* idea that he was here for a concert. I just thought that repulsive collection of slime was here for a publicity visit. And furthermore, what do you intend to do with my limousine?"

I wondered whether he was getting senile. I'd already told him. "I'm going to pick up the missing equipment so the concert can be held tonight. Isn't that a good idea, Mr. Wells? After all, if I may remind you, no instruments, no concert."

"I have no desire to have any such concert take place in MY memorial stadium!" he said.

So I decided to bring out the big guns. "No concert, no hot dogs, no sodas, no popcorn and candy bars . . . need I say more?"

"I don't care about the money," he said after a long time. But I could see that it was hard for him. "And furthermore, I'd rather see the Wells Memorial Stadium BURN to the GROUND . . . than have a rock concert in it! I hate that noise, and I hate the types who go to those concerts even more!"

"If you try and cancel the concert now, Simon Gear will sue—and you'll lose lots and lots of money!" I yelled.

That got him for a second. But then Rufus began to look crafty. "Oh, no, I *want* the concert to go on," he said. "But I don't have to help you find the equipment. That way, if Gear isn't ready to play, I can sue *him*."

"Oh, yeah?" I said. I was getting mad by now. "I bet you're going to burn the stadium down and then collect the insurance on it! You're just the type who would do a thing like that!"

Well, it was the wrong thing to say. One look at R.Z.'s face, and I realized what I'd just done.

He smiled this oily, horrible smile, and said, "I never thought of that! That's a terrific idea." He beamed at me. "You know, young lady. The more I deal with you, the more respect I have for the way

81

your devious little mind works. How old did you say you were?"

Billy was so glad to hear his uncle say something nice about one of his friends, he blurted out, "Minnie's twelve, sir. Just like me!"

I aimed a kick at Billy, but I missed.

R.Z. stood there for a second, rubbing his chin and squinting at me. I couldn't take it anymore.

"Do I get the car, or don't I?" I asked.

"No. You don't," he said. "But come back in ten years, and we'll talk about a job. I could use someone like you around here."

"Oh, yeah?" I was *really* mad, now. I went right up to him and stuck my nose right up to his face. "Well, listen to this, you nasty old man! I've got the chicken pox! And right this second I'm *real, real* contagious! So, let *that* be my little gift to you, sir!"

R.Z. opened his mouth, his cigar dropped onto the carpet, and then he turned and ran. He ran right into his executive bathroom and slammed the door. I heard the thunk, thunk the lock made as the tumblers fell into place. Then he screamed, "Get out of my office, you two troublemakers!"

We decided it might be a good time to leave. So we did.

Chapter 11

"HEY, BILLY," I said as we were going down the elevator. "How far away do you think this Welles-burg place is?"

"Let's go to the gas station and get a map," Billy said. He's pretty clever sometimes. I was sorry I'd almost kicked him.

We stopped at the gas station my father always goes to, and Hank Mullins, who works there, got us a map. We finally found this "Wellesburg," and guess what? It was only about seventy miles away from us.

That meant we could get there in about two hours and get the stuff back to *this* Wellsburg with plenty of time to set up everything for the concert.

"We need the van!" I howled, as we rode down Main Street.

"So, why don't we just go get it?" asked Billy. "We'll pick it up from the gas station, drive it . . ."

". . . across the state, without licenses, while being under age," I said, finishing Billy's sentence. "And we won't get caught if we sit on the telephone books, because the only way the cops will know that we're twelve is because we will be driving all over the road."

"Why are we going to be driving all over the road?" Billy asked.

"Because neither one of us knows how to drive a van, and it has a stick shift, not an automatic, which makes it even worse. That's why."

"I see what you mean," said Billy.

We thought some more.

"We could always go tell Simon Gear that we found the stuff," Billy said. "We could tell him where it is, and then the driver of the tour bus could go pick it up."

"How are we going to do that?" I asked. "Lower ourselves down from the roof on sheets? We can't even get into the hotel, much less up to his room to tell him. They'll never put the calls through, either."

"Ummmmmmmm," said Billy. "Then there's only one answer. We have to get Lennie."

"I know," I said. "But how?"

"We go to his house and we tell him what's been happening, that's how."

"Have you ever been to his house?" I asked.

"No," Billy answered. "I don't even know where it is."

"Let's find a phone book. We'll look up his address in there."

So we did, but his name wasn't there. I called information, and the operator said she had a listing for a Leonard Farini on Oak Road. I called but a recording said the telephone had been disconnected.

"That's okay," I said. "We were planning to pop in, anyway."

Oak Road isn't the nicest area, but Billy and I pedaled as fast as we could. Time was trickling out on us, and we had a mission!

We pulled into Lennie's block, and I looked for a mailbox or something with the name Farini on it. There were mailboxes, but there were no names, just numbers. About three quarters of the way down the street, though, I saw Lennie's motorcycle parked in front of a garage.

The garage door was broken, and the house attached to this garage looked sort of broken too. The screened-in porch was a mess. The screens were all hanging down to the grass—if that's what you want to call it. The house needed a coat of paint. So did the grass.

"I think that's it," I said, pointing to Lennie's

motorcycle. We slowed down and looked to see if anyone was around. But it looked pretty deserted.

"I hope he's home," Billy said.

"How far away could he be?" I said. "Some people never go anyplace without their teddy bears, Lennie never goes anyplace without his motorcycle."

We dropped our bikes in front of the porch and went up the steps. I pulled open the storm door—it had a big hole in the glass—and knocked on the front door.

"What!" yelled a voice from inside. Billy looked at me, and I looked at him. "I don't wanna buy anything!"

"Lennie!" I yelled. "Open up. We have to talk to you."

There was a crash, and a curse, and about two seconds later the door opened.

"What the heck are you two doing here?" Lennie said, as he looked at us in his doorway. "Can't you babies leave me alone?"

"No, we can't," I said. "Lennie, we need you to drive the van."

"I'm not driving your dumb van for you any-more, got it?"

"Lennie, you have to!" I wailed. "You're our only chance!"

"You should have thought of that before you let that half-wit Dave Madison spend all his spare time insulting me. A guy's got pride, you know."

"Lennie, we're sorry about Dave. And besides"—I decided to work in a few half-truths—"Dave quit. He's no longer at the station. Please help us?"

For a minute there I thought Lennie would crack. But he didn't. "Forget it," he said. "I already talked to my parole officer, and he's helping me get a job that pays. I'm finished with you kids. I did my time, and now I'm out." He stepped back and started to close the door.

"Lennie!" I yelled. "PLEE-EE-EE-EASE!"

"See ya round, kid," he said. Then he shut the door.

Billy and I stood on the porch, and then realized that Lennie meant it. No Lennie, no van, no instruments, no concert, no exclusive coverage. Boy, KID-TV was about to really blow it, I thought.

"You know who could make him do it?" Billy said. "Willow. That's who."

"I don't think so," I said. "She wishes she could, but I don't know if Lennie cares much about Willow."

"Let's get her to try," said Billy. "We'll ask her to come here and see what she can do."

"Why not," I said. "We haven't got anything better to do. Except steal a car . . . with automatic shift, of course."

"Minnie!"

"All right, all right," I said as we picked up our bikes. "Let's find a phone booth."

We didn't find a phone booth, but we found a candy store, and the man let us use his telephone for fifty cents. Highway robbery! Anyway, we called the station, and Willow had just gotten back from the hotel. Nothing much was happening there, she told us, so she decided to come back and edit some of the tapes. I told her she couldn't make them any better than they already were.

Then I told her our problem, and begged her to come down to Oak Road and meet us in front of Lennie's house—fast.

She jumped at the chance, as I knew she would. We went back to Lennie's front lawn and sat down leaning against the mailbox post to wait. I checked the house a couple of times, and I thought I saw someone lift a curtain to look out at us. But if it was Lennie, he never came to talk, so we just waited.

We didn't have to wait long.

Willow came flying down the block on her bicycle about fifteen minutes later. As soon as I told her what we needed and what we'd discovered, she was up on Lennie's front porch, pounding away at the door.

Instead of making her stand outside all by her

self, Lennie came out on the porch. That was good, because even though I didn't want to make it look like I was spying on them, I wanted to hear what they said.

First she asked Lennie to do it for KID-TV. But Lennie just laughed at her. Then she asked him to do it for her. He mumbled that even though she was a nice kid, and even though he was sorry to put her through a lot of grief, he still didn't think it would be in his best interests to do it—even for her.

He was pretty nice to her about it, but I still felt crummy. Thank goodness he didn't laugh at her!

Then Willow asked if he would do it for Simon Gear. Lennie really got a howl out of that! He said why should he put himself out for some guy who was that rich and that famous.

Then Willow asked him what he'd consider to be a big enough return. Lennie chuckled, and flexed his muscles, and said he might consider it for one thing. But it was something that she, Willow, couldn't possibly deliver, so why should he even bother to tell her.

Well, Willow couldn't resist. Maybe it was watching Lennie flex his muscles or something. Anyway, Willow said she really wanted to know, because she really respected him, and she really wanted to know just exactly what made him tick.

She said even though she knew she couldn't give him what he wanted, she would still like to know what it was.

And Lennie said he wanted to be rich and famous like Simon Gear so he didn't have to spend all his time dealing with babies like us, and low-life motorcycle gangs.

Then Willow got this big smile on her face, and she got sort of wiggly. She looked at him for a long time, and then she said, "Well, Lennie, I can't make you rich. Only you can do that. But I can make you famous."

"How?" Lennie hooted.

"Lennie, I know I don't have to tell you this," Willow said real slowly. "But you are one incredible hunk. I bet you could make it in the movies, and make it big. Look at Matt Dillon. Why not start your career on KID-TV? Why not start tonight at the concert? You can do the concert coverage, okay? Everyone will be watching because it's Simon Gear."

First Lennie's face fell, and he looked surprised. It was as if someone had just punched him in the stomach. Then he sort of started strutting around the porch a little. He reminded me of a rooster I once saw at the children's zoo in Milwaukee.

"That's right," he said slowly. "This is going to be the only time that everyone around here will be turned in to KID-TV, or at least *lots* of people. This might even be picked up by one of the networks."

"Right, Lennie," Willow said. "But there's one little problem. You see, if we don't go pick up the equipment in the van, there won't be any concert. You can't handle the coverage unless you pick up the instruments. Think about it."

"What's to think about?" Lennie said. He was acting very, very cool. "Let's go."

Willow whooped.

Lennie darted in the door, grabbed his black leather jacket, and took off down the steps to his motorcycle. "Ride on the back, Willow," he said, as he kicked the bike to a start. "We'll pick up the van. Then we'll head out to the throughway!"

"What about us!" I screeched.

"You go to the hotel, and tell Simon Gear that we're on the way to get his stuff," yelled Willow. "We'll pick you guys up there in half an hour."

The motorcycle roared off down the street. Billy and I jumped on our bikes, and headed for the Wellsburg Arms.

"How do we know that Jamie will let Lennie do the coverage?" I called to Billy as we went around the corner and out onto Main Street.

"Once she knows why, she'll let him do anything," Billy yelled back. "And besides, Willow is right. Lennie would be really great on camera.

He'd be a lot better than any of the dingdongs we have now—except Willow of course!"

Billy was right. Lennie was a natural. I wondered how come we'd never thought of it before.

Chapter 12

FROM HERE ON in, it should have been a cinch, right? We should have just popped over to the hotel, told Simon about how we found his equipment and were going to pick it up. Then he would have groveled and kissed our hands and feet in gratitude, and then we would have driven to this Wellesburg place and gotten the equipment, brought it back, and set it up. Right?

Wrong.

We got to the hotel and found that we'd managed to cut our own throats.

Every Simon Gear fan for a hundred miles in every direction had seen the KID-TV coverage. They had, of course, found out the name of the hotel where he was staying, thanks to Lance and Mike McGee. So, of course, the next thing they'd done

BARBARA ADAMS

was show up to mob the street, the sidewalk in front, and everything for fourteen blocks in every direction.

Police, extra guards, and every doorman who had ever worked at the Wellsburg Arms Hotel was standing outside, covering every entrance, and making sure that nobody, but nobody, got into the hotel.

Of course, our hopes for a scoop were gone as well. Dozens of newspaper photographers were fighting their way through the mob, plus four television camera crews—one with our friend Bob Appleman. Bob is a local TV newsman who's given us lots of help since KID-TV started. Jamie has a crush on Bob—I could see her looking over at him with this goofy smile on her face.

One good thing—the grown-up news teams weren't having any better luck than we did with the hotel people. *Nobody* was getting in.

But the KID-TV staff was still trying. We had inherited all the costumes from the Wallinsky Wax Museum when it closed. Until now we'd never figured out what to use them for. Now was the chance. While Billy and I had been busy with R.Z. and Lennie, the rest of the staff had been busy with the costumes.

I've said a lot of things about the KID-TV staff, but I *never* said they were uncreative.

ROCK VIDEO STRIKES AGAIN

I would need an awful lot more room to tell you what exactly they did, but let me try and run it by you as quickly as possible. Because when we got there it was like something out of a Marx brothers movie.

First, it took them an awful lot of shoving and pushing to get to where the staff had their cameras set up. Rock Video was there, announcing every ten seconds that he was the press. He *demanded* the right to get into the hotel. Of course, they didn't believe him. So that was that. He was getting pushed and shoved and jostled and elbowed like everybody else.

Jamie had summoned Lance and Jeannie back to the hotel. Lance, who had decided that being sneaky was the only plan worth discussing, had chosen a Napoleon uniform from the Wax Museum. It was a perfect fit—just right for someone short and dumpy.

Using this Napoleon costume to disguise himself as a bellboy, Lance tried to get into the lobby through the service entrance pushing what was supposed to be one of those carts they use to deliver meals for room service.

He'd cleverly hidden Jeannie under the table—which, by the way, was his mother's mahogany dinner cart. He'd stolen it from their dining room—and covered it with a tablecloth. The tablecloth was a monogrammed linen one from his mother's special trousseau trunk. I got to see what was left of it after he was thrown out of the hotel. I expect that Lance will soon be minus an arm at the very least.

Anyway, he and Jeannie actually got as far as the elevators before they were stopped by private house detectives. That was because Lance was pushing the cart a little too fast. When he went around the corner, Jeannie started to stick out. Oh, well.

Then, Dave Madison, who is always creative, dressed as himself, tried to check in as a traveling salesman. He "borrowed" his father's attaché case, and filled his mother's suitcase with newspapers and bricks. He slicked his hair back with some grease—don't ask me why because I've never seen a salesman who looked as yucky as Dave did—and he got as far as the front desk.

But it seems that he also "borrowed" his father's American Express card. When he had to sign the voucher, instead of signing it Robert Walpole Madison, he signed it Dave Madison.

They threw him out too.

Which brings us to Muffin and her disguise. She got the Mata Hari costume out of the storeroom. In case you didn't know, Mata Hari was this really slick woman spy in World War One. The costume looked like something a belly dancer would wear, with a lacy veil over it. Muffin's other great trick of disguise was to have a huge mound of gum in her mouth.

Billy and I got there just in time to see her launch her attack on the hotel security. Muffin walked up, snapping her fingers and her gum in tempo. "Well, the Material Girl is here," she told the doorman. "Flew in all the way from the coast to sing with my man Simon. So where is he?"

But the doorman wasn't as dumb as he looked—which wasn't too dumb. All he said was, "That's funny, you look just like the kid that does the exercises on TV every afternoon—the one with the big ears."

Muffin staggered off. It looked like she was trying to make up her mind. Should she be pleased at having a grown-up fan? Or annoyed over that crack about her ears?

Well, they may have been playing around, but I, Minnie O'Reilly, was serious. I had a definite message to get to the star. So I just marched right up and tried to tell a policeman that I needed an escort into the hotel to deliver a vital message to Simon Gear.

He told me to write a letter.

How dumb can you get!

I tried to get to Jamie, but she was mobbed by a bunch of teenagers who were waving at their mothers or something. I tried waving too, just to get her attention. But as I mentioned earlier, I'm short. One of these days, I'm going to be tall—then watch out, guys. I've had it with this kind of discrimination!

It was no use. I was getting shoved farther and farther away from the front of the hotel. I couldn't even get close to the sidewalk much less get inside the lobby! Then I saw some of the roadies that had been on the bus scurrying out the back way.

Now's my chance, I thought, and I sprinted across the parking lot . . . just in time to see them get into a car.

"Hey! Wait!" I yelled. "I gotta talk to you a minute!"

The big, tinted window rolled down for a second, and this odd-looking girl stuck her head out. Her hair was purple and green and yellow.

"Don't get yourself a heart attack," she yelled to me. "Simon is planning to cancel the stupid concert anyway!"

"But . . . but I know where the equipment . . ."

The tinted window rolled up, and the car pulled out onto Maple Street.

I sat down in the middle of the lot. What was I going to do? If Simon canceled the concert, then it wouldn't matter whether he got the equipment or not. All he had to know was that it was coming in time. Then he wouldn't cancel, Rock would get his video, KID-TV would do the coverage we'd promised, and everything would be fine.

But no one would listen to me. There was no way to tell these turkeys anything. I wished I was a grown-up.

That was the first time I'd ever wished for anything so insane in my life. Being a grown-up could only be slightly worse than being a teenager—which was slightly worse than being deaf and dumb. The only good thing about being a grown-up was that other grown-ups listened to you. They trusted you. They also saw you when you stood in front of them.

That was my only objection to being a kid. It was like being invisible. Mostly that was good, but . . .

"Hey wait a minute!" I said out loud to the lamp post. "That's the answer."

Now I knew exactly what to do. I stood up, turned around, got on my bike, and headed home.

Four minutes later I pulled into the driveway, dropped my bike on top of Ron's—which was still lying in the azalea bushes—and tore into the house.

Once up the stairs, I quietly closed the door to my room. I didn't want Ron sniffing around. Then I opened my closet.

There it was! My horrible yellow dress. The one

with the short skirt, the pleats, and the little yellow rose at the waist.

Aaargh.

It was the one my mother always made me wear
when I went to the Garden Club luncheons with
her. I hated that dress because it made me look two
years younger.

But today was different. Today I *wanted* to look
two years younger. I needed to be invisible today.

I took off my jeans and put on the stupid dress,
the black patent-leather Mary Janes, and short
white socks with yellow roses embroidered around
the tops. Yeck.

I put my hair up in two ponytails—one over
each ear—and stuck those yellow plastic bird bar-
rettes over the rubber bands. Barf.

I was ready!

Careful not to get bicycle grease on my stupid
socks, I pedaled back to the hotel as fast as I could.

There wasn't much time, because Lennie and
Willow were going to meet us in front of the hotel.
I thought maybe I'd try and find Billy to warn
him, but then I thought better of it. Billy would
know what to do, just in case I missed them all.
He could tell them to wait for me. And if they
wouldn't—well, so what.

He knew where the equipment was. My job was
just as important. I *had* to keep Simon Gear from

canceling this concert if it was the last thing I did.

I walked the bike around the hotel to the side entrance. After leaning against the wall, I carefully walked up to the door next to the kitchens.

There was this great big guy standing there with his arms crossed over his chest. He looked like one of his sneezes would topple the Empire State Building. Then I put this really dumb look on my face and worked up a good lisp.

"Exthcuthe me thir," I said with a real stuck-up little-girl voice, "but I have to get in to thee my daddy. He told me to meet him in the lobby."

"Sure thing, kid," he said. He didn't even look at me! He just opened the door and I walked right by him. "Go straight ahead and take the elevator to your left."

"Thankth," I said, and I was IN!

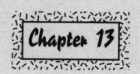

Chapter 13

I TOOK THE elevator to the lobby and I glanced around. There wasn't too much happening. Some newspaper guys and TV crew were hanging around in there looking bored.

I walked right up to one of the newspaper guys and put on my best lisp. "Excusth me, mithter. I'm looking for my daddy. He thaid to meet him in the lobby."

"You better go over to the desk, kid," said the man. "This place is a mob scene because of Simon Gear."

"Who'th he?" I said.

The guy laughed. "Who's he? Who's he? He's just this rock star that all the kids love. Never heard of him?"

"Nope," I said. "I jutht want to find my daddy. Ith thith rock thtar in the lobby?"

"Naw, kid," said the man. "He's up in the tenth-floor suite. I'm afraid you won't get to see him."

"Who careth," I said.

Whoopee! He'd told me exactly what I wanted to know. I walked over toward the desk, just in case the newsman was still watching me. Halfway there I changed direction and made a dash for the stairs. It would be safer to walk up than try to convince some elevator man to let me off on the tenth floor.

The only thing that had me worried was the chicken pox. What if Simon hadn't had the pox? What if I gave it to him? But then there was KID-TV to think about too. I was the only one who'd gotten this far. I had to make sure the concert went on tonight. It *had* to! "Just remember not to breathe on him," I told myself, running upstairs as fast as I could.

By the sixth floor I was winded and had to sit down. But only for a minute. Once I'd caught my breath, I kept going.

At the tenth-floor landing, I opened the door a crack, just to see how heavily it was guarded.

There was one guy sitting outside one of the doors. He had hair down to his shoulders, wore three earrings in one ear, and was fast asleep.

That's probably the door to the tenth-floor suite, I thought. And that banana is probably the faithful watchman.

My kind of watchman, I thought. I walked down the hall, stepped over the sleeping guard, and banged on the door.

I waited a couple of seconds and then decided I'd better bang again, quick. After all, even though the watchman looked as if he'd died four hours ago, he might still wake up before I got anyone to answer the door.

So I banged *really* hard—as if the hotel was burning down or something. That got results.

The door was flung open, and there I was, standing face to face with Simon Gear himself. From twenty feet he was good—but from one foot he was even better! That's when I remembered about my disease.

"Have you ever had the chicken pox?" I asked, quick.

He just looked at me as if I'd landed from Mars. He was about to open his mouth and yell something—I could tell by the way his eyebrows were getting closer and closer to his chin—when I decided I'd better talk fast and forget the chicken pox.

"Look, Mr. Gear," I said, quickly pushing past him and getting myself inside the room. Boy, was it a mess! "I've had a terrible time getting up here to see you, but I have some infor—"

"I don't care what you have, kid!" he yelled. "I wish I'd never agreed to this insane trip. It's been nothing but garbage, aggravation, and lunacy since we got here!"

"Yeah, but—" I said, trying to sound reasonable.

"Yeah, but nothing," he yelled. "I'm sick of this town, I'm sick of this concert, and I'm sick of idiots like you trying to get at me so they can tear my shirt off!"

"I don't want to tear your shirt off," I said. I was getting annoyed. "All I want is to tell you . . ."

"Don't tell me anything, kid," he snapped. " 'Cause I don't want to hear it!"

He turned away from me, and I could see into the room better. It was like a whole apartment, but without the kitchen. There were ashtrays all over the place, and open suitcases with clothes spilling out of them, and magazines lying open everywhere. Two television sets were on, tuned to two different soap operas.

The rest of Simon's group was sitting around— but not on the things you're supposed to sit on. They were sitting on the bureau, the television set, the floor. And through the open door of the bathroom I could see one of them sitting on the sink. I wondered if there was anything wrong with the chairs in this hotel. I decided to mention it to Willow—maybe there was a story here.

I was about to give Simon Gear a piece of my mind, when we heard a commotion in the street. Screams and sirens and strange wailing noises. It sounded as if there was a riot going on out there.

The guy with the straw hair ran to the window and pushed it open. Simon and I got there just in time to see what the trouble was.

The trouble was Rock Video. He was out on the ledge, glued to the brick wall, with his video camera hanging around his neck.

He was frozen with terror.

"What the—" said Simon Gear.

"Hey, Rock," I called out to him. "Why don't you come in here? That's a stupid place to stand."

Rock said, "Glugh, glugh, glugh." I think he was so afraid to move any part of himself that he was afraid to move his lips too.

"Don't just stand out there going 'glugh, glugh,'" I said, taking command of the situation. "I want you to grab hold of my hand, and then I'll help you get in the window. . . . And stop looking down. It's not helping you any."

Rock dragged his eyes away from the street, and I could tell he had focused them fuzzily on the water tank on top of the building across the way.

Simon and his group just stood and gaped. I jabbed my elbow into Simon's ribs.

"Oof!" he said.

"Hold on to me, dummy," I growled. Then I climbed out on the window sill. Kneeling as far out as I could without falling, I held my hand out to Rock. By now someone was holding on to my waist with both hands. That was very good, because when I looked down, I didn't feel so good myself.

"Now, Rock," I said, trying to sound very calm, "I want you to slide your left foot along the ledge . . . just a little bit at a time."

Rock said, "Glugh!" and slid his foot about two inches.

"That's real good," I said. "Keep your hands flat against the building, just like they are now. That's perfect. Now slide your other foot a bit to catch up. . . . Good. Perfect. Now slide your left foot again, and you'll be able to reach my hand."

"Mumphle," said Rock, but he did what I told him to do.

"You don't have to look for my hand," I said, "because I can see yours." I kept talking because I thought maybe the sound of my voice would calm him down so he could move. "Just keep your eyes on that water tower. I'll grab your hand when you slide just a little bit more. . . . Great! I've got your hand. Just stay there for a second. I've got you, so now you're safe. Rest for a second."

He was squeezing my hand so hard, I thought he'd mash all my fingers. I quickly turned my head and whispered to Simon Gear.

"Now, hold on to me, real tight, because I have to lean way out, and give him both my hands. . . . And get someone else to lean out too. When he gets opposite the window, we'll grab him and pull him in."

Simon Gear held on to me, and the guy with the leather vest and the dark hair held on to him. I think that was Chick. The guy with the straw hair leaned out next to me, and one of the girls in the group held on to him.

"Just a couple more slides," I said to Rock. And Rock gurgled and slid . . . right in front of the window.

We grabbed him and yanked him inside.

We all fell in a heap on the floor. Fortunately I was close to the top of the heap so it wasn't too bad.

We lay there for a couple of seconds, and then the guy on the bottom, the dark-haired one who'd been holding on to Simon Gear, started to yell. He gave a big shove, and the heap fell apart. We all scrambled to our feet except Rock Video. He was lying flat on his back with his eyes wide open.

"That was brave, kid," Simon Gear said to me. "I thought for sure this banana was either going to jump or fall."

"Thank you," I said, trying to look humble.

"Where did you learn how to talk someone off a ledge?" he asked.

"From television, of course," I said. "Where else? You think they teach that stuff in sixth grade?"

Simon nodded and then turned his attention back to Rock Video—who hadn't moved yet, or blinked.

"What the heck were you trying to prove?" Simon Gear asked him. But Rock kept on staring, and didn't answer.

I gave him a little nudge in the leg with my patent-leather Mary Janes. "Speak up, Rock. We can't hear a word you're saying."

Rock blinked a couple of times, and then he slowly sat up. "I gotta check my lenses," he said. "If these got broken I'm up the creek. They're my last ones."

"Oh, no!" yelled Simon Gear. "Another nut with a camera! Get him out of here, Bennie!"

"Wait a second," I said. "First of all, we're not nuts. We want to get an interview and make a video. We're from KID-TV, and we have a lot riding on this interview."

"I don't care about your problem, kid," he said,

109

staring at me. "This idiot almost killed himself outside my window! The publicity would have been horrible . . . terrible! It could have ruined my career. The absolutely last person I'd give an interview to is that stupid kid!"

"Oh, yeah?" I said. Then I turned back to Rock. "Start rolling your camera, buddy. I want you to capture this moment for all Simon Gear's fans. I want them all to see how mean he is to the very people who put him on the map!"

Rock held his camera up, and started rolling. For some reason or other, I had the feeling Simon Gear didn't like that. He started to stalk out of the room, and I knew I had to do something tough, or we'd lose the moment we'd managed to steal.

So, I stuck my foot out and tripped him.

Chapter 14

FORTUNATELY, THE STAR didn't hurt himself. He fell onto the couch. He was about to get up, but I blocked his escape route.

"Now listen here," I said, putting my hands on my hips. "You've got a lot of nerve, mister. I just came up here to tell you that I found your stupid equipment, and I'm about to go get it for you!"

"Yeah?" he said, looking surprised. "Where'd you find it?"

"In Wellesburg, naturally," I said. "Where else would it be? It just doesn't happen to be in *this* Wellsburg is all. In case you're interested, there are an awful lot of Wellsburgs."

"I'm beginning to get the picture," he said.

"Anyhow," I continued, "I found the stupid stuff, and I'm bringing it to the stupid stadium for

111

you, and if you don't stop screaming at us . . . I won't! And I won't tell which Wellsburg it's in, either. . . . And good luck finding it yourself, buddy!"

"You wouldn't . . ." said the guy with the straw hair. He looked worried. Hah!

"You bet I would," I said. "You know, it's not *our* fault this isn't your stupid hometown, and it's not *our* fault that your manager turned out to be a birdbrain. So don't take it out on us, okay?"

I thought I heard a muttered "Okay," but I wasn't sure. So I turned around, still blocking his escape route by wedging myself in between the coffee table and the wall. I stuck my nose in the air and waited for an apology.

After a couple of seconds I peeked out of the corner of my eye. Luckily, he was looking a little sorry. So I stuck my nose higher.

"Look, I'm awfully sorry," he said after a while. "It's just that everything's been so messed up, I'm in a foul mood."

"I'll say," I said. "By the way, my name is Minnie O'Reilly, and this is Rock Video."

"How do you do," he said. "This is my band. This is Chick, and Bennie, and Weasel, and Airy Mary, and Moxie."

He waved his hand around. I couldn't tell which name went with which person, except maybe I figured the girl was named Airy Mary. After all, that sounds like a girl's name. But you never know. Maybe the straw-haired guy was Airy Mary and the girl was named Weasel . . . or Bennie.

"How do you do," I said. "Now, can I use your phone, please?"

"Sure."

Before he could think about it, I called downstairs, and told the desk man that Mr. Gear in the tenth-floor suite needed to speak with the crew from KID-TV. Could he please get the doorman to escort them upstairs immediately?

I hung up before Simon Gear could scream, and then I said, "I think it's about time you started to set up the arrangements for the concert with my people. Since we're the ones making it possible, it's the least you can do. After all, no concert, no money, right?"

"Wrong," said Simon Gear. "I'm not making money on this concert. I was going to give the money to charity."

"Hey, neat," I said. "Which charity?"

Simon looked a little embarrassed. "I'm not sure," he answered, looking like he'd rather be someplace else right now. "I was going to pick out a worthy charity once we got here, but then . . . Well, you saw what happened with my manager."

"No problem," I said. My mind was suddenly

113

whirring away. "Do you mind if the charity isn't one in your *real* hometown, but one in *this* Wellsburg? Because I know just the place."

"You do?" he said. "No, I don't mind at all. What place did you have in mind . . . and don't tell me it's the Minnie O'Reilly College and Candy Fund."

I gave him a dirty look. "Don't be stupid," I said. "It's the Hollingswood Children's Hospital. They got caught in all the federal cutbacks, and they've lost their funding. They need money something terrible."

"That sounds real good," Simon said, brightening up a lot. "I could make the announcement tonight at the concert!"

"I have a better idea," I said. "Make the announcement right now. The concert will be a total sellout, and furthermore, once we get 'em all inside the stadium, we could ask people to give extra donations at the door during the intermission!"

"Not bad," he said thoughtfully. "Where'd you learn how to do fund raising? They don't teach *that* on television, do they?"

"Nope, I'm a natural," I said.

Just then there was pounding on the door, and before anyone could open it, it flew open all by itself. Well, not exactly. That watchman, the sleeping one, was awake now—sort of. He'd opened the door to warn Simon that a bunch of crazies were on the floor. But it was too late. The whole KID-TV staff had barreled right over him and they were standing in the room.

Some of them were still wearing their idiotic costumes, which was the thing that had gotten the watch dog so upset. Not that I blame him. I wouldn't have let them in my suite, either. At least not looking like that.

Dave looked a little surprised to see Rock Video. "Hey kid," he said, "I see you decided not to end your poor pitiful life."

"Dave!" Jamie said.

"I wasn't committing suicide, you ninny," Rock muttered while he turned beet red. "I was using an old trick to get in here to see Simon Gear. I was planning to take a video through the window."

"Oh, too bad," said Dave. "Well, better luck next time."

"Can't get better than it already is," Rock said, the red fading, and a smile pulling up the corners of his lips. "I'm getting a video right this second, right?"

Sandy, who was dressed as Rona Barrett—which was pretty much the way she dressed normally— pushed Dave aside. She held out a big mail sack and said, "Simon, I have all your love letters!"

"I never wrote you any love letters," he said, looking horrified. "I never even saw you before!"

"Not from me, silly," Sandy cooed. "From your fans!"

Simon Gear looked relieved. "Oh. Yeah. Right. Just put 'em someplace."

Before anybody else could interrupt, I introduced the KID-TV staff to the rock group. Even though Simon looked a bit skeptical about who they all were (the costumes were truly strange) he was nice.

Muffin started twitching and wriggling, but Dave Madison was the worst. He explained to Simon how he was going to invest the profit from the concert in shopping malls across the nation. He was just launching into the return-on-investment picture when Jamie elbowed him out of the way and told him to be quiet. Boy, was he getting his lumps from ladies today!

Jamie told Simon Gear that we'd love to have an exclusive interview with him down at the KID-TV studio after the concert.

Simon looked gloomy for about half a second, and then he said, "Okay, I don't normally do that sort of thing, but I think this little girl is outa sight!"

"What a nice thing to say!" Jamie said. "We all think she's outa sight, too, don't we?"

Billy beamed, and I guess I did too.

But I thought Muffin was going to spit, and

Dave looked stunned. He started to speak, but I stepped on his foot. These Mary Janes aren't bad as weapons, I thought to myself as Dave doubled over and grabbed his foot. He was still wearing his sneakers with his traveling salesman outfit.

"And I've decided to donate the proceeds from the concert to the . . . what's it called, Minnie?" he said.

"The Hollingswood Children's Hospital," I said. "And he'd like to make the announcement now."

"That's right," Simon said.

"Rock, could you please get a tape of this, because Willow isn't here right now."

"Great idea," Jamie said. "We'll run the announcement on KID-TV this afternoon. That way everyone will know what your plan is."

"And we'd like to collect donations during the intermission," I said. "Maybe you could ask for volunteers to collect the money for us while you're at it."

"Isn't she terrific?" Simon said, looking right at me. I had a small fit of dizziness, because even though I'm not the type who gets excited about rock stars, it was kind of exciting to have such a famous person say such great things about me. And I had to admit, he was awfully good-looking!

I was feeling very pleased with myself, when Billy tapped me on the shoulder.

"It's been forty-five minutes," he whispered.

"Forty-five minutes till what?" I whispered back.

That's when I remembered that I'd forgotten all about Lennie and Willow waiting for us in the van.

"Omigosh!" I said. "Lennie and Willow!"

"Lennie?" said Dave, looking irritated. "What does Lennie have to do with us?"

"A lot," I said, giving him the fish-eye. "No thanks to you. Lennie has agreed to drive the van to Wellesburg to get the equipment."

"You actually found the equipment?" gasped Jamie. "How did you do that?"

"We borrowed Uncle Rufus's phone and called every Wellsburg in the country," Billy said. "We finally found the stuff across the state!"

Everyone started buzzing and cheering. "And not only that," I said. "Lennie has agreed to come back to KID-TV. Willow said he could do the coverage of the concert himself!"

Jamie looked stunned, but then her expression began to change. It went from stunned to thoughtful, past suspicious, and then directly into delighted.

"What a great idea!" she said. "Lennie is obviously the best person we could have chosen. . . . He has presence . . . he has bone structure . . ."

"And he can see without glasses," I said. "Besides, it was the only deal he would take, so forget about the presence and the bone structure and the glasses. It wouldn't have mattered if he looked like a frog."

"He'll be pur-r-r . . . fect," Muffin purred. That glazed expression was coming on her face. Uh, oh, I thought. Watch out, Lennie. Here comes Muffin.

The poor guy, I wonder how he'll get that one off his ankle. Once she thinks he's a film star—of sorts—there'll be no stopping her. But I had to chuckle. If I thought Lennie was going to be mad, I could just see how mad Muffin's father was going to be. After all, Miss Prendergast of the Prendergast Potato Chip fortune was supposed to hang out with college men. Not graduates of the Williston Home for Wayward Boys!

But enough of this. I had places to go, things to do, people to see! I, Minnie O'Reilly, was needed elsewhere!

"Listen, folks," I said. "I have to get downstairs in a hurry and make sure we get this stuff back here and set up in time for the concert tonight."

"Good work!" Jamie said. "Minnie, we all appreciate everything you've done today."

"That wasn't all she did," said Simon Gear. "She also saved that kid with the camera. She climbed right out the window and brought him inside. I was really impressed. She's spunky. A little mean, maybe . . . but really spunky."

I started to give him another dirty look, but decided it was a backhanded compliment.

"C'mon, Billy," I said. "Let's get this show on the road."

"Yeah," said Simon Gear. "And let's clear this place out too. I've got to get a little rest. After all, I have a concert to do tonight!"

He was gently pushing everyone toward the door when Rock Video spoke up.

"I'll just stay for three minutes and get your taped announcement about the proceeds of the concert, okay?"

"Okay," said Simon. "But the rest of you—amscray."

"Whaddiddeesay?" mumbled Dave as we backed out of the suite.

"That's pig Latin for 'Scram,' dummy," I said when we got out into the hall.

"Wow," said Dave. "I didn't know he was an intellectual too!"

As Billy and I ran down the stairs, I wondered what rock we'd found Dave Madison under.

Chapter 15

"WHERE THE HECK have you two been!" Lennie howled when we got down to the van. "Billy said he'd be five minutes, and we've been sitting here for twenty!"

"Keep your shirt on," I snapped. "I was lining up an interview, making a video, and saving Rock from the window ledge."

"It's true," said Billy, as he pulled open the side door of the van. I climbed inside, and he came in after me. "Rock Video was on the tenth-floor ledge outside Simon Gear's window, and he froze."

"So he was cold," Lennie muttered as he put the van in gear. Billy and I were in the back with the equipment, and Willow was sitting up front with Lennie. "Big deal. He should have worn a sweater."

"Drive the truck, Lennie," I said. "When a person

121

is out on a ledge, and someone says 'He froze,' they mean he couldn't move."

Lennie didn't answer right away. Then he said, "I knew that. I was just teasing you."

"Right," I replied. "Now did anyone remember to bring the map that shows us how to get to this Wellesburg place?"

"Of course," said Lennie. "Who do you think is in charge here?"

I could see he already thought of himself as a star, and was going to be even harder to take than before.

Lennie drove through town, and then got onto the throughway. I checked my watch and saw that it was a little before two thirty. That meant we'd be in Wellesburg by four thirty, pick up the stuff, and get to the stadium by six thirty. The concert was at eight thirty, so we had plenty of time. It couldn't take more than an hour to set up the equipment, so I decided I could relax a bit. After all, I thought, stratching my shoulder, I'm supposed to be sick.

I found a clear space on the floor of the van and leaned back against the side. Lennie had rock music blaring out of the radio, but I didn't mind. I didn't want to sleep—I just wanted to think. I wanted to wallow in peace and quiet for a change.

What a day it had been! Between getting up

early for the pleasure of watching Simon Gear fire his manager, watching the KID-TV staff behave like bananas—with the exception of Jamie and Willow, of course—conning Uncle Rufus, making a hundred and twenty telephone calls, tracking down Lennie and persuading him to return, and then saving Rock's life on the ledge, I figured it was time for some quiet. Whew!

Great in theory, but not in practice. There I was relaxing, listening to the music, and generally having a pleasant time of it, when suddenly the van started to swerve all over the road.

Willow screamed, Lennie swore, and Billy looked as if he was about to be sick.

I was about to die.

My life flashed before my eyes. I thought about my wonderful mother and father, and my dear, sweet brother Ron.

Well . . . let's not go *that* far. But I must say, when on the brink of death, I didn't think he was quite as bubbleheaded as I do now.

That's right. You guessed it. I lived to tell the tale. You see, the van had gotten a flat tire. And at the speed that Lennie usually travels, this was quite an event. Fortunately there was no other car close enough for us to hit. So after sailing all across three lanes, and then back, we bumped along the grassy shoulder until the van came to a stop.

I felt myself all over to make sure nothing was broken, and then, because I wasn't yet sure what had happened, I started yelling.

"Lennie, you maniac!" I screeched. "Who told you to drive like that! What happened? What did you do now? Whatever it was, I don't wanna hear about it! Don't do it again!"

"Hush, babykins," he said, opening the door to the van. "Keep your shirt on." I hate it when people use your own lines on you. "We got a flat."

"Oh, Lennie, that was so masterful," Willow cooed. "I never thought you'd be able to save us from that skid."

We never would have been *in* that skid, I thought, if he hadn't been driving so fast! Anyone with half a brain knows that when you get a blowout at high speeds, you can't control the car at all. I learned *that* on television too. I watch Driver Education on Saturday mornings at six A.M.

Just as an unrelated comment, I think that's a dumb time to air a show that almost everyone needs to see. They should have it on at six o'clock in the evening instead of the news. I mean, half the people in this country drive as if they'd gotten their licenses off cereal boxes. They really *need* that show, not kids who get up early!

Anyway, after examining the damage, Lennie came back to report that the tire was totally wrecked, and so was the rim. So that meant we'd have to drive the rest of the way on the spare—which meant that if we got another flat tire we were doomed.

And what was worse, he wanted *us* to change the tire because he didn't want to get dirty!

"The original greaser doesn't want to get greasy?" I muttered.

But Willow said that was right, because Lennie would have to go right on the air as soon as we got back to the Wellsburg we all know and love. I had to admit she was right. We were going to lose a half an hour at least! Oh, well.

So there we were, changing the tire while Lennie sat on the grass chewing a piece of hay and giving us instructions. Aaargh!

He seemed to think it was pretty cute, but I, Minnie O'Reilly, thought it was dumb.

However, I thought to myself as I unscrewed the fifth lug bolt, think of this as a way of getting experience. After all, I never paid any attention while Dad changed a tire, so who knew what had to be done. Part of my education as a self-sufficient female person was a definite need to know how to change a tire.

Of course, my mother would have gone nuts if she saw me doing such a thing in my yellow dress. But, I thought happily, while wiping a greasy hand on my skirt, this may mean the last of this dopey dress. It's about time, too.

Anyway, we were back on the road again in twenty-five minutes, and on our way. Now, you would think that after that experience Lennie would try driving at the speed limit, right? Wrong. He was cruising at seventy, with his head swiveling around like a lighthouse beacon, watching for the police cars.

That would be all we needed now, I thought miserably. To get pulled over by a cop, who would find a van driven by a parolee, start asking questions, and blow our schedule completely!

I crossed my fingers and prayed.

And my prayers were answered . . . sort of. We didn't get pulled over by a cop. We got stuck behind a wide-load hay truck on the narrow, two-lane road going into this Wellesburg place. The hay wagon was going fifteen miles an hour!

Lennie honked. Willow and I screamed. Billy even swore (I was impressed by his range of subject matter).

But did it do any good? Nope.

The wagon finally pulled off onto an even smaller road about five miles and thirty minutes later.

We'd already lost about an hour by the time we got to the bus depot in Wellesburg. But the guy there was really nice, and even helped us load the van. I signed for the stuff, and then off we drove back home.

By this time, there was no room in the back of the van, so Billy had to sit in the middle and I had to sit on Willow's lap. How humiliating!

And dangerous, too. Every time we went over a bump, I banged my head on the roof of the van. If we had hit one more pothole, I would have had to unbutton my blouse to brush my teeth!

I was getting really itchy, too. But it was so crowded up there, I couldn't reach around and scratch. I finally had to ask Willow if she would scratch my back for me.

"I know this sounds disgusting," I said. "But my chicken pox is getting out of hand, and I need you to scratch it for me, Willow."

"WHAT!" yelled Lennie. "You didn't tell me that kid was sick!"

He almost drove the van off the road, he was so upset.

"Didn't you have the chicken pox in second grade?" I asked. "Everybody else did."

"How the heck would I know," he wailed. I was interested that he was so tough, but he still was scared of germs. What a baby!

"Well," Billy said, "it's too late now. You've already been in the van with her for hours. If you haven't had it yet, you've already been exposed."

"But don't worry," I added. "I looked it up, and the incubation period is fourteen days. That means no one will think you've got acne for at least two weeks!"

Meanwhile, Willow had been scratching my shoulder. "Is that the only place it itches?" she asked.

"Yes."

"That's odd," she said. "I thought you were supposed to get the spots all over your back and chest. Do you mind if I take a look?"

Well, I made Billy close his eyes, and I told Lennie to keep his eyes on the road, and I let Willow unzip the back of my dress so she could look.

"That's not chicken pox!" she said. "That's a mosquito bite!"

Chapter 16

"Fantastic!" I yelled. "Are you sure?"

"Positive," said Willow.

"Saved," said Lennie.

"Too bad you didn't know before this," said Billy.

"Who cares," said I. "I'm celebrating!"

And I sang along with the radio all the way into Wellsburg . . . even when the others begged me to stop.

When we got into the stadium at a quarter to eight, everyone was there waiting for us. As we pulled the van into the loading bay, they cheered and started unloading. We had the equipment set up in half an hour because we had so many helpers, and the concert started right on schedule.

The whole time we were working, Lennie was in the bathroom combing his hair. It's a wonder he could hold his head up, he had so much grease on it. But when he went out to introduce the band, he was great! Even I, Minnie O'Reilly, was surprised. He really *did* have stage presence! Jamie started talking about giving him a talk show to go along with Rock Video's video.

A booming voice cut across the backstage bustle. "Let me through, I say!" I recognized the voice immediately. R.Z. Wells.

Rufus the Doofus came up to Jamie, saying, "I'd like to go on stage, with a few words." He rattled what looked like thirty-five typewritten sheets in his hand. "After all, the Hollingswood Children's Hospital has always been one of my favorite charities."

"I heard that you cut them off without a dime when they wouldn't change their name to the Wells Children's Hospital," I muttered. Rufus heard me and gave me a dirty look.

"Right now might not be the best time for a long speech, Mr. Wells," Jamie said, more tactfully. "The fans are very eager for the music to begin."

That was an understatement. Lennie had the kids in the seats chanting, "Simon! Simon! SI-mon! SI-MON *SI-MON*!"

Rufus went pale as he heard that. I think he realized he might be lynched if he held up the concert.

ROCK VIDEO STRIKES AGAIN

It was a concert too. Not only that, the volunteers collected three thousand dollars for the Hollingswood Children's Hospital—and that was on top of the box office take! Not bad, right? Right.

Rock Video was all set up right before the footlights on the stage. He got the absolute best, clearest video of a concert I've ever seen.

On top of that, Simon Gear wore a KID-TV sweatshirt to do the concert instead of his regular costume. I think that was a particularly wise move on his part, since his regular costume is awfully weird. I mean, the pants were too tight, and the vest has feathers and sequins on it! Aaargh. I think he should wear our sweatshirt at all his concerts, and I told him so.

The best part of all was that at the end of the show, when everyone was clapping and screaming for more, Simon Gear took the mike and said, "Folks, this has been a great concert, and you've been a fantastic audience. But it never could have taken place at all without the help of a great kid who lives right here in your town."

And then, would you believe? He called me—me, Minnie O'Reilly—right up there on stage with him!

"Minnie O'Reilly is the one who saved my equipment, saved my concert, and helped me raise this money for the Hollingswood Children's Hospital. I think she deserves a great big hand from all of you!"

There I was in my dippy yellow dress with oil stains on it, my hair like a bird's nest, five thousand people in the stadium cheering and clapping, just for me! Well, all except one. R.Z. Wells still stood backstage, with his speech all squashed up in his hands. He never did get to give it.

Up until then, it was perfect. But after that, it got sloppy. Simon sang this really sappy love song right at me. I could have died. I've never been so embarrassed in my whole life!

The only thing that made it acceptable was that I *knew* Muffin Prendergast was positively green.

You know how I know? She hasn't spoken to me since. What a relief! If I had nothing else to thank Simon Gear for, I would still be in his debt for saving me from Muffin's little tips on hair and makeup: "You could minimize your pointy chin if you cut your hair a little shorter." "Sometimes small eyes can be made to look bigger if you put eyeliner on the bottom lid, but not the top one."

Not only are her comments sort of insulting, but they're probably the opposite of good advice, if you know what I mean.

When I got home, my whole family was sitting up beside the television. Dad gave me a kiss and told me what a great job I had done. Mom was a little ticked off about what had happened to my yellow dress. And Ron—well, he looked even sicker than when he found out he had chicken pox. Sick with jealousy. I had been on TV, with a rock star, and he had missed it *all*!

The next day was even better, if you can believe such a thing.

As he had promised Jamie, Simon Gear came to the studio Sunday for an exclusive interview for KID-TV. But when he got there, instead of letting Lance or Lennie do the interview . . . he demanded me! Me, Minnie O'Reilly! I got the best shot at stardom of all! For a whole half hour I got to ask Simon Gear all about himself and his career. And guess what? I even found out where he was from.

Of course, you already know. He's from Wellsburg.

Aha! But which one? Well, the answer turned out to be none.

Simon had called his mother before the concert, and she'd told him that they'd voted to change the name of his hometown last year. Are you ready for this? They changed it to Gearsville—and they never told him!

Right before the interview, Rock gave us a preview of his video. It was a little weird, but Simon Gear was nice about it. He said, "I see you're still into New Wave."

Whatever that means.

This is what Rock's video was: tops of heads, sides of cars, sickening views out the tenth floor window of the Wellsburg Arms Hotel, chair legs, people legs, dog legs, and a little bit of the rock group. He cut it up a bit so at the end, you have Simon Gear smiling and laughing, and then it goes into the beginning of the concert.

In a way the video really was pretty good. You see, it ended up being the story of his home-coming concert, and if you can stand back and look at the whole thing objectively, it was a funny story. The sound track is all Simon Gear's songs, and it was like that old Beatles movie *A Hard Day's Night*. You know, everyone running around and speeded-up parts with people's feet moving too fast.

Surprise of surprises, Simon Gear liked it. He even said he'd put his other rock musician friends in touch with KID-TV for exclusive interviews and video made by Rock Video himself.

Right before he left, he shook everyone's hand, gave me a kiss, and even signed his autograph on Muffin's arm!

You know what I think? I think that girl has no class at all. That is what I, personally, think.

So you can see that we were all in seventh heaven. That's what my grandmother always says. But she usually says it about desserts, not about professional situations.

It was all we could do to keep our minds on the planning meeting for the next week of shows. After all, we were about to become the Phil Donahue show of rock. We were all about to be rich and famous!

"It's a good thing I set this whole thing up for you guys," Dave Madison said. "Although it was a pure stroke of luck that Simon's manager walked off the job, it was a pure stroke of genius on his part to hire me as his temporary replacement! We got tons of ads, thanks to my hard work—and once I get the figures together, I bet we'll have enough to buy a new camera. I tell you, without me, this entire tiddlywink operation would fold."

"Dave!" Lennie said sweetly, "go stick your head in the toilet three times and take it out twice!"

"Lennie," yelled Dave, "you're fired!"

"He is not!" yelled Willow.

They were fighting again, and so I tried to break it up. I yelled, "KID-TV lives!" But they were making too much noise.

Even though this day was the first day of the rest of our future glorious lives, you can see that it didn't take us too long to get back to normal!

So then I yelled. "Hey! Anybody want any baby gerbils? They make great pets!" Nobody answered.

Oh, well. Maybe I should try selling them for outrageous prices. People are always more interested in expensive items than free ones.

See you later, fans! And remember, KID-TV lives. Tell everybody.

PATRICIA REILLY GIFF

writes about girls and boys just like you:

- clever
- cheerful
- stubborn
- mad
- brainy
- average
- happy
- sad

Show your parents this list of her funny, serious, wonderful books
—to own, read, and treasure for years!

____ FOURTH GRADE CELEBRITY	42676-6	$2.50
____ GIFT OF THE PIRATE QUEEN	43046-1	2.75
____ THE GIRL WHO KNEW IT ALL ...	42855-6	2.50
____ HAVE YOU SEEN HYACINTH MACAW	43450-5	2.50
____ LEFT-HANDED SHORTSTOP	44672-4	2.50
____ LORETTA P. SWEENY, WHERE ARE YOU?	44926-X	2.50
____ RAT TEETH	47457-4	2.50
____ WINTER WORM BUSINESS	49259-9	2.50

Yearling Books

At your local bookstore or use this handy coupon for ordering:

DELL READERS SERVICE—DEPT. A98D
P.O. BOX 1000, PINE BROOK, N.J. 07058

Please send me the above title(s). I am enclosing $_____ (please add 75¢ per copy to cover postage and handling.) Send check or money order—no cash or CODs. Please allow 3-4 weeks for shipment.

Name_____

Address_____

City_____ State/Zip_____